Second Workshop on Automatic Simultaneous Translation Challenges, Recent Advances, and Future Directions 2021

Online
10 June 2021

ISBN: 978-1-7138-3016-0

Printed from e-media with permission by:

Curran Associates, Inc.
57 Morehouse Lane
Red Hook, NY 12571

Some format issues inherent in the e-media version may also appear in this print version.

Printed with permission by Curran Associates, Inc. (2021)

For permission requests, please contact the Association for Computational Linguistics at the address below.

Association for Computational Linguistics
209 N. Eighth Street
Stroudsburg, Pennsylvania 18360

Phone: 1-570-476-8006
Fax: 1-570-476-0860

acl@aclweb.org

Additional copies of this publication are available from:

Curran Associates, Inc.
57 Morehouse Lane
Red Hook, NY 12571 USA
Phone: 845-758-0400
Fax: 845-758-2633
Email: curran@proceedings.com
Web: www.proceedings.com

NAACL-HLT 2021

Automatic Simultaneous Translation
Challenges, Recent Advances, and Future Directions

The Proceedings of the Second Workshop

June, 10, 2021

Introduction

Welcome to the Second Workshop on Automatic Simultaneous Translation (AutoSimTrans)! Simultaneous translation, which performs translation concurrently with the source speech, is widely useful in many scenarios such as international conferences, negotiations, press releases, legal proceedings, and medicine. It combines the AI technologies of machine translation (MT), automatic speech recognition (ASR), and text-to-speech synthesis (TTS), which is becoming a cutting-edge research field.

As an emerging and interdisciplinary field, simultaneous translation faces many great challenges and is considered one of the holy grails of AI. This workshop will bring together researchers and practitioners in machine translation, speech processing, and human interpretation, to discuss recent advances and open challenges of simultaneous translation.

We organized a simultaneous translation shared task on Chinese-English. We released a dataset for open research, which covers speeches in a wide range of domains, such as IT, economy, culture, biology, arts, etc.

Following the tradition of our first workshop, we will have two sets of keynote speakers: Will Lewis, Lucia Specia, and Liang Huang from simultaneous translation, and Hong Jiang from human interpretation research. We hope this workshop will greatly increase the communication and cross-fertilization between the two fields. We have accepted 6 papers that will be presented in the second session.

We look forward to an exciting workshop!

Hua Wu, Colin Cherry, Liang Huang, Zhongjun He, Qun Liu, Maha Elbayad, Mark Liberman, and Haifeng Wang

Organizers:

Hua Wu, Baidu Inc.
Colin Cherry, Google
Liang Huang, Oregon State University and Baidu Research
Zhongjun He, Baidu Inc.
Qun Liu, Huawei Noah's Ark Lab
Maha Elbayad, Université Grenoble Alpes

Steering Committee:

Mark Liberman, University of Pennsylvania
Haifeng Wang, Baidu Inc.

Program Chair:

Mingbo Ma, Baidu Research, USA

Shared Task Chair:

Ruiqing Zhang, Baidu Inc.

Program Committee:

Naveen Arivazhagan, Google, USA
Chung-Cheng Chiu, Google, USA
Kenneth Church, Baidu Research, USA
Yang Feng, CAS/ICT, China
George Foster, Google, Canada
Alvin Grissom II, Ursinus College, USA
He He, NYU, USA
Alina Karakanta, FBK-Trento, Italy
Wei Li, Google, USA
Hairong Liu, Baidu Research, USA
Kaibo Liu, Baidu Research, USA
Wolfgang Macherey, Google, USA
Jan Niehues, Maastricht U., Netherlands
Yusuke Oda, Google, Japan
Colin Raffel, Google, USA
Elizabeth Salesky, CMU, USA
Jiajun Zhang, CAS/IA, China
Renjie Zheng, Oregon State Univ., USA

Invited Speakers:

Will Lewis, Affiliate Faculty, University of Washington
Lucia Specia, Professor, Imperial College London, UK
Liang Huang, Assoc. Professor, Oregon State and Distinguished Scientist, Baidu Research, USA
Hong Jiang, Sr. Lecturer, Dept. of Translation, Chinese University of Hong Kong, China

Table of Contents

Conference Program

Thursday, June 10, 2021 (all time in PST)

07:15–07:30 *Opening Remarks*

07:30–10:10 **Session 1 Invited Talks**

07:30–08:10 *Invited Talk by Hong Jiang*

08:10–08:50 *Invited Talk by Lucia Specia*

08:50–09:30 *Invited Talk by Liang Huang*

09:30–10:10 *Invited Talk by Will Lewis*

10:10–19:00 **Break**

19:00–20:20 **Session 2: Research Paper and System Description**

19:00–19:10 *ICT's System for AutoSimTrans 2021: Robust Char-Level Simultaneous Translation*
Shaolei Zhang and Yang Feng

19:10–19:20 *BIT's system for AutoSimulTrans2021*
Mengge Liu, Shuoying Chen, Minqin Li, Zhipeng Wang and Yuhang Guo

19:20–19:30 *XMU's Simultaneous Translation System at NAACL 2021*
Shuangtao Li, Jinming Hu, Boli Wang, Xiaodong Shi and Yidong Chen

19:30–19:40 *System Description on Automatic Simultaneous Translation Workshop*
Linjie Chen, Jianzong Wang, Zhangcheng Huang, Xiongbin Ding and Jing Xiao

19:40–19:50 *BSTC: A Large-Scale Chinese-English Speech Translation Dataset*
Ruiqing Zhang, Xiyang Wang, Chuanqiang Zhang, Zhongjun He, Hua Wu, Zhi Li, Haifeng Wang, Ying Chen and Qinfei Li

Thursday, June 10, 2021 (all time in PST) (continued)

19:50–20:00 *Findings of the Second Workshop on Automatic Simultaneous Translation*
Ruiqing Zhang, Chuanqiang Zhang, Zhongjun He, Hua Wu and Haifeng Wang

20:00–20:20 *Q&A*

20:20–20:30 ***Closing Remarks***

ICT's System for AutoSimTrans 2021: Robust Char-Level Simultaneous Translation

Shaolei Zhang [1,2], **Yang Feng** [1,2*]
[1]Key Laboratory of Intelligent Information Processing
Institute of Computing Technology, Chinese Academy of Sciences (ICT/CAS)
[2] University of Chinese Academy of Sciences, Beijing, China
{zhangshaolei20z, fengyang}@ ict.ac.cn

Abstract

Simultaneous translation (ST) outputs the translation simultaneously while reading the input sentence, which is an important component of simultaneous interpretation. In this paper, we describe our submitted ST system, which won the first place in the streaming transcription input track of the Chinese-English translation task of AutoSimTrans 2021. Aiming at the robustness of ST, we first propose char-level simultaneous translation and applied wait-k policy on it. Meanwhile, we apply two data processing methods and combine two training methods for domain adaptation. Our method enhance the ST model with stronger robustness and domain adaptability. Experiments on streaming transcription show that our method outperforms the baseline at all latency, especially at low latency, the proposed method improves about 6 BLEU. Besides, ablation studies we conduct verify the effectiveness of each module in the proposed method.

1 Introduction

Automatic simultaneous translation (ST) (Cho and Esipova, 2016; Gu et al., 2017; Ma et al., 2019), a task in machine translation (MT), aims to output the target translation while reading the source sentence. The standard machine translation is a full-sentence MT, which waits for the complete source input and then starts translation. The huge latency caused by full-sentence MT is unacceptable in many real-time scenarios. On the contrary, ST is widely used in real simultaneous speech translation scenarios, such as simultaneous interpretation, synchronized subtitles, and live broadcasting.

Previous methods (Ma et al., 2019; Arivazhagan et al., 2019) for ST are all evaluated on the existing full-sentence MT parallel corpus, ignoring the real speech translation scenario. In the real scene, the paradigm of simultaneous interpretation is Automatic Speech Recognition (ASR) $\rightarrow$ simultaneous translation (ST) $\rightarrow$ Text-to-Speech Synthesis (TTS), in which these three parts are all carried out simultaneously. As a downstream task of simultaneous ASR, the input of ST is always not exactly correct and in the spoken language domain. Thus, robustness and domain adaptability become two challenges for the ST system.

For robustness, since the input of the ST system is ASR result (streaming transcription), which is incremental and may be unsegmented or incorrectly segmented, the subword-level segmentation result (Ma et al., 2019) of the streaming transcription seriously affect the ST result. Existing methods (Li et al., 2020) often remove the last token after segmentation to prevent it from being incomplete, which leads to a considerable increase in latency. Table 1 shows an example of the tokenization result of the streaming transcription input with different methods. In steps 4-7 of standard wait-2, the input prefix is different from its previous step, while the previous output prefix is not allowed to be modified in ST, which leads to serious translation errors. Although removing the last token improves the robustness, there is no new input in many consecutive steps, which greatly increases the latency.

For domain adaptability, the existing spoken language domain corpus is lacking, while the general domain corpus for MT and the spoken language domain corpus for ST are quite different in terms of word order, punctuation and modal particles, so ST needs to efficiently complete the domain adaption.

In our system, we propose a *Char-Level Wait-k Policy* for simultaneous translation, which is more robust with streaming transcription input. Besides, we apply data augmentation and combine two training methods to train the model to complete domain adaptation. Specifically, the source of the char-level wait-k policy is a character sequence segmented according to characters, and the target still maintains subword-level segmentation and BPE operations (Sennrich et al., 2016). When decoding,

*Corresponding author: Yang Feng.

Proceedings of the 2nd Workshop on Automatic Simultaneous Translation, pages 1–11
June 10, 2021. ©2021 Association for Computational Linguistics

Streaming Transcription	Tokenization of Streaming Transcription Input		
	Standard Wait-2	Standard Wait-2 Remove Last Token	Char-Level Wait-2 (Ours)
他是研究生物的			
他是研究生物的	他 / 是 /	他 /	他 / 是 /
他是研究生物的	他 / 是 / 研 /	他 / 是 / ▷ Delay	他 / 是 / 研 /
他是研究生物的	他 / 是 / 研究 / ✘	他 / 是 / ▷ Delay	他 / 是 / 研 / 究 /
他是研究生物的	他 / 是 / 研究生 / ✘	他 / 是 / ▷ Delay	他 / 是 / 研 / 究 / 生 /
他是研究生物的	他 / 是 / 研究 / 生物 / ✘	他 / 是 / 研究 /	他 / 是 / 研 / 究 / 生 / 物 /
他是研究生物的	他 / 是 / 研究 / 生物 / 的 /	他 / 是 / 研究 / 生物 / 的 /	他 / 是 / 研 / 究 / 生 / 物 / 的 /

Table 1: An example of the tokenization result of standard wait-k, standard wait-k+remove last token and char-level wait-k, when dealing with streaming transcription input (take $k = 2$ as an example). Red mark: the source prefix changes during streaming input. Green mark: no input in consecutive steps since the last token is removed.

the char-level wait-k policy first waits for k source characters, then alternately reads a character, and outputs a target subword. Table 1 shows the tokenization results of the char-level wait-k policy, which not only guarantees the stability of the input prefix but also avoids unnecessary latency. To adapt to the spoken language domain, we first pretrain an ST model on the general domain corpus and perform fine-tuning on the spoken language domain corpus. To improve the effect and efficiency of domain adaptation, we carry out data augmentation on both the general domain corpus and spoken language domain corpus and combine two different training methods for training.

In the streaming transcription track for the Chinese → English translation task of AutoSimTrans 2021, we evaluate the proposed method on the real speech corpus (Zhang et al., 2021). Our method exceeds the baseline model at all latency and performs more prominently at lower latency.

Our contributions can be summarized as follows:

- To our best knowledge, we are the first to propose char-level simultaneous translation, which is more robust when dealing with real streaming input.
- We apply data augmentation and incorporate two training methods, which effectively improve the domain adaptation and overcome the shortage of spoken language corpus.

2 Task Description

We participated in the streaming transcription input track of the Chinese-English translation task of AutoSimTrans 2021 [1]. An example of the task

Streaming Transcript	Translation
大	
大家	
大家好	Hello everyone!
欢	
欢迎	
欢迎大	
欢迎大家	
欢迎大家来	Welcome
欢迎大家来到	everyone
欢迎大家来到这	come
欢迎大家来到这里	here.

Table 2: An example of streaming transcription output track of the Chinese-English translation task.

is shown in Table 2. Streaming transcription is manually transcribed without word segmentation. Between each step, the source input adds one more character. The task applies AL and BLEU respectively to evaluate the latency and translation quality of the submitted system.

3 Background

Our system is based on a variant of wait-k policy (Ma et al., 2019), so we first briefly introduce wait-k policy and its training method.

Wait-k policy refers to waiting for k source tokens first, and then reading and writing alternately, i.e., the output always delays k tokens after the input. As shown by 'standard wait-k policy' in Figure 1, if $k = 2$, the first target token was output after reading 2 source tokens, and then output a target token as soon as a source token is read.

Define $g(t)$ as a monotonic non-decreasing function of t, which represents the number of source

[1] https://autosimtrans.github.io/shared

tokens read in when outputting the target token y_t. For the wait-k policy, $g(t)$ is calculated as:

$$g(t) = \min\{k + t - 1, |\boldsymbol{x}|\}, t = 1, 2, \cdots \quad (1)$$

where $\boldsymbol{x}$ is the input subword sequence.

Wait-k policy is trained with "prefix-to-prefix" framework. In "prefix-to-prefix" framework, when generating the tth target word, the source tokens participating in encoder is limited to less than $g(t)$.

4 Methods

To improve the robustness and domain adaptability of ST, we enhance our system from read / write policy, data processing and training methods respectively.

4.1 Char-Level Wait-k Policy

To enhance the robustness of dealing with streaming transcription, we first proposed char-level simultaneous translation and applied the wait-k policy on it.

4.1.1 Char-Level Simultaneous Translation

Character-level neural machine translation (Ling et al., 2015; Lee et al., 2017; Cherry et al., 2018; Gao et al., 2020) tokenizes the source sentence and target sentence according to characters, thereby gaining advantages over subword-level neural machine translation in some specific aspects, such as avoiding out-of-vocabulary problems (Passban et al., 2018) and errors caused by subword-level segmentation (Tang et al., 2020). In terms of translation quality, the character-level MT is still difficult to compare with the subword-level MT. An important reason is that only one wrong generated character will directly cause the entire target word wrong (Sennrich, 2017).

To improve the robustness of the ST system when dealing with unsegmented incremental input, while avoiding the performance degradation caused by character-level MT, we propose *char-level simultaneous translation*, which is more suitable for streaming input. The framework of char-level ST is shown in the lower part of Figure 1.

Different from subword-level ST, given the parallel sentence pair $< X, Y >$, the source of the ST model in the proposed char-level ST is the character sequence $\boldsymbol{c} = (c_1, \cdots, c_n)$ after char-level tokenization, and the target is the subword sequence $\boldsymbol{y} = (y_1, \cdots, y_m)$ after word segmentation and BPE (Sennrich et al., 2016), where n and m are the source and target sequence lengths respectively.

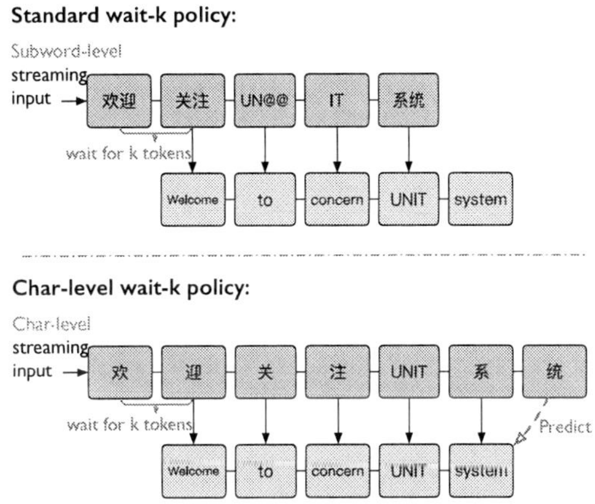

Figure 1: Standard wait-k policy vs. our char-level wait-k policy (take $k = 2$ as an example).

The word segmentation and BPE operation at the target end are the same as subword-level MT (Vaswani et al., 2017), and char-level tokenization is similar to character-level MT (Yang et al., 2016; Nikolov et al., 2018; Saunders et al., 2020) but not completely consistent. The char-level tokenization we proposed divides each source language character into a token, and other characters (such as numbers, other language characters) are still divided into a token according to complete words. An example of char-level tokenization is shown in Table 3. In the result of char-level tokenization, each Chinese character is divided into a token, and the number (12) and English (UNIT) are entirely taken as a token, respectively. Char-level tokenization is more suitable for streaming transcription, which ensures that the newly input content at each step in streaming transcription is a complete token, and the input prefix does not change in any way. The robustness of char-level ST is greatly improved with the complete token and stable prefix.

Why char-level simultaneous translation? Motivating our use of char-level ST we consider three desiderata. 1) With the incremental source input, char-level ST is more robust since it avoids unstable prefixes caused by word segmentation, as shown in Table 1. 2) Char-level ST can obtain a more fine-grained latency, because if one character is enough to express the meaning of a entire word, the ST system does not have to wait for the complete word before translating. 3) Char-level ST only performs char-level tokenization on the source, while the target still retains subword-level tokenization, so its translation performance will not be affected too much, as shown in Table 7.

Input Sentence		欢迎来到UNIT系统的第12期高级课程。
Output Sentence		welcome to the 12th advanced course on UNIT system .
S.	subword-level MT	欢迎 / 来到 / UN@@ / IT / 系统 / 的 / 第 / 12@@ / 期 / 高级 / 课程 / 。
	character-level MT	欢 / 迎 / 来 / 到 / U / N / I / T / 系 / 统 / 的 / 第 / 1 / 2 / 期 / 高 / 级 / 课 / 程 / 。
	char-level tokenization	欢 / 迎 / 来 / 到 / UNIT / 系 / 统 / 的 / 第 / 12 / 期 / 高 / 级 / 课 / 程 / 。
T.	subword-level MT	welcome / to / the / 12@@ / th / advanced / course / on / UNIT / system / .

Table 3: An example of tokenization method applied by the char-level wait-k policy. For the source, we use char-level tokenization, which separates each source language character into separate segments, and divides the others by words. For the target, we apply the same operation as the conventional subword-level MT. The sentences marked in red are the source and target of our proposed ST model.

4.1.2 Read / Write Policy

For the read / write policy, we apply the wait-k policy on the proposed char-level ST. The difference between char-level wait-k policy and standard wait-k policy is that each token in standard wait-k policy is a subword, while each token in char-level wait-k policy is a character (other languages or Numbers are still words), as shown in Figure 1.

We rewrite $g(t)$ in Eq.(1) into $g_k(t)$ for char-level wait-k policy, which represents the number of source tokens (Character) read in when outputting the target token y_t, calculated as:

$$g_k(t) = \min\{k + t - 1, |\mathbf{c}|\}, t = 1, 2, \cdots \quad (2)$$

where $\mathbf{c}$ is the input character sequence.

Another significant advantage of the standard wait-k policy is that it can obtain some implicit prediction ability in training, and char-level wait-k policy further strengthens the prediction ability and improves the stability of prediction. The reason is that the granularity of the char-level is smaller so that the prediction of char-level is simpler and more accurate than that of subword-level. As shown in Figure 1, it is much simpler and more accurate to predict "系统" given "系", since there are few possible characters that can be followed by "系".

4.2 Domain Adaptation

To improve the quality of domain adaptation, we apply some modifications to all training corpus, including general domain and spoken language domain, to make them more closer to streaming transcription. Besides, we also augment the spoken language corpus to make up for the lack of data.

4.2.1 Depunctuation

For training corpus, including general domain and spoken language domain, the most serious difference from streaming transcription is that each sentence in streaming transcription usually lacks ending punctuation, as shown in Table 2. Since the punctuation in the training corpus is complete, and the ending punctuation is often followed by $< eos >$, the model trained with them tends to wait for the source ending punctuation and then generate the corresponding target ending punctuation and $< eos >$ to stop translating. As a result, given the unpunctuated input in streaming transcription, it is difficult for the model to generate target punctuation and $< eos >$ to stop the translation.

Original	各位开发者、各位朋友们，大家下午好！
Depunctuation	各位开发者、各位朋友们，大家下午好

Table 4: An example of depunctuation operation, where the ending punctuation of the source sentence is deleted.

To this end, to strengthen the model's ability to translate punctuation from unpunctuated sentences, we delete the ending punctuation of the source sentence, and the target sentence remains unchanged, as shown in Table 4. Note that our depunctuation operation is limited to the ending punctuation at the end of the source sentence ('。','！','？').

4.2.2 Data Augmentation

For the spoken language domain corpus, since the data size is too small, we perform data augmentation on the source sentence. For each source sentence, we perform 5 operations: add a comma, add a tone character, copy an adjacent character, replace a character with its homophone, or delete a character. Meanwhile, the target sentence remains unchanged. The proposed method improves the robustness of the model while augmenting the data. An example of data augmentation is shown in Table 5.

Original	1957年我到北京上大学
Add Comma	1957年，我到北京上大学
Add Tone character	1957年我啊到北京上大学
Copy Character	1957年我到北北京上大学
Replace Homophone	1957年我到北经上大学
Delete Character	1957年我到北京上大学

Table 5: An example of data augmentation.

4.3 Training Methods

Our method is based on Transformer (Vaswani et al., 2017), and the training is divided into two stages. First, we pre-train an ST model on the general domain MT corpus, and then fine-tune the ST model on the spoken language domain corpus. For pre-training, we apply *multi-path* (Elbayad et al., 2020) and *future-guided* (Zhang et al., 2020b), to enhance the predict ability and avoid the huge consumption caused by training different models for each k. For fine-tuning, we apply the original prefix-to-prefix framework (Ma et al., 2019).

4.3.1 Pre-training

To improve the predictive ability of the ST model, we apply the future-guided training proposed by (Zhang et al., 2020b). Besides the incremental Transformer for simultaneous translation with char-level wait-k policy, we introduce a full-sentence Transformer, used as the teacher of the incremental Transformer for ST through knowledge distillation. The full-sentence Transformer is trained with cross-entropy loss:

$$\mathcal{L}(\theta_{full}) = -\sum_{(\mathbf{c},\mathbf{y})\in D_g}\sum_{t=1}^{|\mathbf{y}|}\log p_{\theta_{full}}(y_t \mid \mathbf{y}_{<t}, \mathbf{c}) \tag{3}$$

where θ_{full} is the parameter of full-sentence Transformer, D_g is the general domain corpus.

For the incremental Transformer for ST, since it applies char-level wait-k policy, the source tokens participating in translating are limited to less than $g_k(t)$ when decoding the tth target token. For each k, the decoding probability is calculated as:

$$p(\mathbf{y} \mid \mathbf{c}, k) = \prod_{t=1}^{|\mathbf{y}|} p_{\theta_{incr}}\left(y_t \mid \mathbf{y}_{<t}, \mathbf{c}_{\leq g_k(t)}\right) \tag{4}$$

where $\mathbf{c}$ and $\mathbf{y}$ are the input character sequence and the output subword sequence, respectively. $\mathbf{c}_{\leq g_k(t)}$ represents the first $g_k(t)$ tokens of $\mathbf{c}$. θ_{incr} is the parameter of incremental Transformer.

Following Elbayad et al. (2020), to cover all possible k during training, we apply multi-path training. k is not fixed during training, but randomly and uniformly sampled from K, where $K = [1, \cdots, |\mathbf{c}|]$ is the set of all possible values of k. Incremental Transformer is also trained with cross-entropy loss:

$$\mathcal{L}(\theta_{incr}) = -\sum_{(\mathbf{c},\mathbf{y})\in D_g}\sum_{t=1,k\sim\mathcal{U}(\mathrm{K})}^{|\mathbf{y}|}\log p_{\theta_{incr}}\left(y_t \mid \mathbf{y}_{<t}, \mathbf{c}_{\leq g_k(t)}\right) \tag{5}$$

For the knowledge distillation between full-sentence Transformer and incremental Transformer, we apply L_2 regularization term between their encoder hidden states, calculated as:

$$\mathcal{L}\left(\mathbf{z}^{incr}, \mathbf{z}^{full}\right) = \frac{1}{|\mathbf{c}|}\sum_{i=1}^{|\mathbf{c}|}\left\|z_i^{incr} - z_i^{full}\right\|^2 \tag{6}$$

where $\mathbf{z}^{incr}$ and $\mathbf{z}^{full}$ represent the hidden states of incremental Transformer and full-sentence Transformer, respectively.

Finally, the total loss $\mathcal{L}$ is calculated as:

$$\mathcal{L} = \mathcal{L}(\theta_{incr}) + \mathcal{L}(\theta_{full}) + \lambda\mathcal{L}\left(\mathbf{z}^{incr}, \mathbf{z}^{full}\right) \tag{7}$$

where λ is the hyper-parameter, and we set $\lambda = 0.1$ in our system.

4.3.2 Fine-tuning

After pre-training an ST model, we use spoken language domain corpus for fine-tuning. The spoken language domain corpus is a small dataset, and meanwhile most of the word order between the target and the source is the same, so we do not continue to use multi-path and future-guided training methods. We fix k and use the original prefix-to-prefix framework for training, and train different models for each k. Given k, the incremental Transformer is trained with cross-entropy loss:

$$\mathcal{L}(\theta_{incr}, k) = -\sum_{(\mathbf{c},\mathbf{y})\in D_s}\sum_{t=1,}^{|\mathbf{y}|}\log p_{\theta_{incr}}\left(y_t \mid \mathbf{y}_{<t}, \mathbf{c}_{\leq g_k(t)}\right) \tag{8}$$

where D_s is the spoken language domain corpus. Finally, for each k, we fine-tuned a ST model.

Datasets	Domain	#Sentence Pairs
CWMT19	General	9,023,708
Transcription	Spoken	37,901
Dev. Set	Spoken	956

Table 6: Statistics of Chinese → English datasets.

5 Experiments

5.1 Dataset

The dataset for Chinese → English task provided by the organizer contains three parts, shown in Table 6. **CWMT19** [2] is the general domain corpus that consists of 9,023,708 sentence pairs. **Transcription** consists of 37,901 sentence pairs and **Dev. Set** consists of 956 sentence pairs [3], which are both spoken language domain corpus collected from real speeches (Zhang et al., 2021).

We use **CWMT19** to pre-train the ST model, then use **Transcription** for fine-tuning, and finally evaluate the latency and translation quality of our system on **Dev. Set**. Note that we use the streaming transcription provided by the organizer for testing. Streaming transcription consists of 23,836 lines, which are composed by breaking each sentence in **Dev. Set** into lines whose length is incremented by one word until the end of the sentence.

We eliminate the corpus with a huge ratio in length between source and target from **CWMT19**, and finally got 8,646,245 pairs of clean corpus. We augment the **Transcription** data according to the method in Sec.4.2.2, and get 227,406 sentence pairs. Meanwhile, for both **CWMT19** and **Transcription**, we remove the ending punctuation according to the method in Sec.4.2.1.

Given the processed corpus after cleaning and augmentation, we first perform char-level tokenization (Sec.4.1) on the Chinese sentences, and tokenize and lowercase English sentences with the Moses[4]. We apply BPE (Sennrich et al., 2016) with 16K merge operations on English.

5.2 System Setting

We set the standard wait-k policy as the baseline and compare our method with it. We conducted experiments on the following systems:

[2]casia2015, casict2011, casict2015, datum2015, datum2017 and neu2017. http://mteval.cipsc.org.cn:81/agreement/AutoSimTrans

[3]https://dataset-bj.cdn.bcebos.com/qianyan%2FAST_Challenge.zip

[4]http://www.statmt.org/moses/

		AL	BLEU	
			Greedy	Beam4
subword level	Pre-train	24.93	20.24	20.35
	+ FT	24.93	24.79	25.39
char level	Pre-train	24.93	20.14	20.28
	+ FT	24.93	24.60	25.13

Table 7: Results of offline model. '+FT': +fine-tuning.

Offline: offline model, full-sentence MT based on Transformer. We report the results of the subword-level / char-level offline model with greedy / beam search respectively in Table 7.

Standard Wait-k: standard subword-level wait-k policy proposed by Ma et al. (2019), used as our baseline. For comparison, we apply the same training method as our method (Sec.4.3) to train it.

Standard Wait-k + rm Last Token: standard subword-level wait-k policy. In the inference time, the last token after the word segmentation is remove to prevent it from being incomplete.

Char-Level Wait-k: our proposed method, refer to Sec.4 for details.

The implementation of all systems is based on Transformer-Big, and adapted from Fairseq Library (Ott et al., 2019). The parameters are the same as the original Transformer (Vaswani et al., 2017). All systems are trained on 4 RTX-3090 GPUs.

5.3 Evaluation Metric

For evaluation metric, we use BLEU [5] (Papineni et al., 2002) and AL[6] (Ma et al., 2019) to measure translation quality and latency, respectively.

Latency metric AL of char-level wait-k policy is calculated with $g_k(t)$ in Eq.(2):

$$\mathrm{AL} = \frac{1}{\tau}\sum_{t=1}^{\tau} g_k(t) - \frac{t-1}{\frac{|\mathbf{y}|}{|\mathbf{c}|}} \tag{9}$$

$$\text{where } \tau = \operatorname*{argmax}_{t}\left(g_k(t) = |\mathbf{c}|\right) \tag{10}$$

where $\mathbf{c}$ and $\mathbf{y}$ are the input character sequence and the output subword sequence, respectively. Note that since the streaming transcription provided by the organizer adds a source character at each step, for all systems, we use character-level AL to evaluate the latency.

[5]The script for calculating BLEU is provided by the organizer from https://dataset-bj.cdn.bcebos.com/qianyan%2FAST_Challenge.zip.

[6]The calculation of AL is as https://github.com/autosimtrans/SimulTransBaseline/blob/master/latency.py.

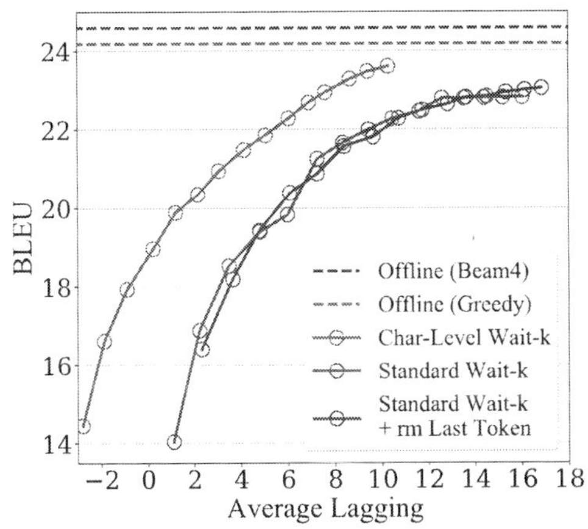

Figure 2: Translation quality (BLEU) against latency (AL) on Chinese → English simultaneous translation, showing the results of proposed char-level wait-k, standard wait-k, standard wait-k+rm last token and offline model with greedy/beam search.

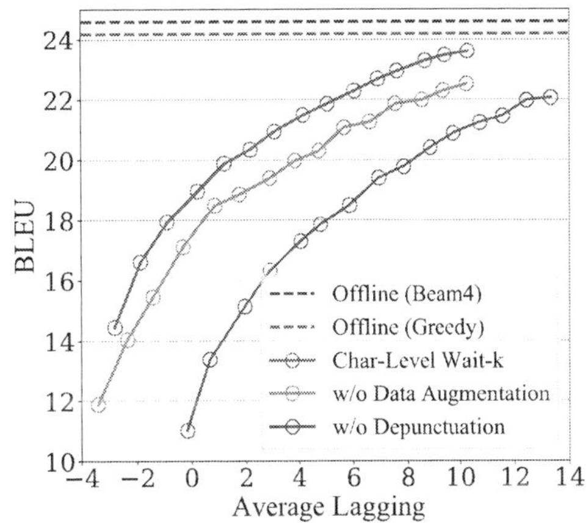

Figure 3: Result of our method without depunctuation or data augmentation.

5.4 Main Result

We compared the performance of our proposed char-level wait-k policy and subword-level wait-k policy, and set $k = 1, 2, \ldots, 15$ to draw the curve of translation quality against latency, as shown in Figure 2. Note that the same value of k for char-level wait-k policy and subword-level wait-k policy does not mean that the latency of the two are similar, because lagging k tokens in char-level wait-k means strictly waiting for k characters, while for subword-level wait-k, it waits for k subwords, which contain more characters.

'Char-Level Wait-k' outperforms 'Standard Wait-k' and 'Standard Wait-k+rm Last Token' at all latency, and improves about 6 BLEU at low latency (AL=1.10). Besides, char-level wait-k performs more stable and robust than standard wait-k when dealing with streaming transcription input, because char-level wait-k has a stable prefix while the prefix of standard wait-k may change between adjacent steps due to the different word segmentation results. 'Standard Wait-k+rm Last Token' solves the issue that the last token may be incomplete, so that the translation quality is higher than Standard Wait-k under the same k, which improves about 0.56 BLEU (average on all k). However, 'Standard Wait-k+rm Last Token' increases the latency. Compared with 'Standard Wait-k', it waits for one more token on average under the same k. Therefore, from the overall curve, the improvement of 'Standard Wait-k+rm Last Token' is limited.

Char-level wait-k is particularly outstanding at low latency, and it achieves good translation quality even when the AL is less than 0. It is worth mentioning that the reason why the AL is less than 0 is that the generated translation is shorter and $\frac{|y|}{|c|}$ in Eq.(9) is greater than 1.

5.5 Effect of Data Processing

To analyze the effect of data processing, including 'Depunctuation' and 'Data Augmentation', we show the results without them in Figure 3.

We notice that data augmentation improves the translation quality of the model by 1.61 BLEU (average on all k), and the model becomes more stable and robust. 'Depunctation' is even more important. If we keep the ending punctuation in the training corpus, the translation quality of the model drops by 2.27 BLEU, and the latency increase by 2.83 (average on all k). This is because streaming transcription input has no ending punctuation, which makes the model hard to generate target ending punctuation and tend to translate longer translations since it is difficult to generate $< eos >$ without target ending punctuation.

5.6 Ablation Study on Training Methods

To enhance the performance and robustness under low latency, we combine future-guided and multipath training methods in pre-training. To verify the effectiveness of the two training methods, we conducted an ablation study on them, and show the results of removing one of them in Figure 4.

When removing one of them, the translation quality decreases, especially at low latency. When the 'Future-guided' is removed, the translation quality decreases by 1.49 BLEU (average on all

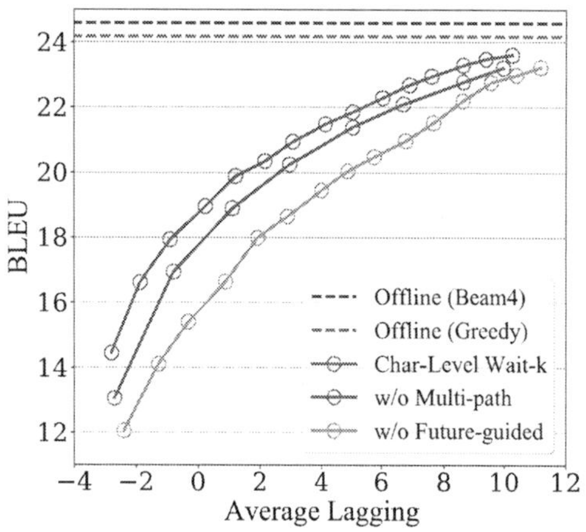

Figure 4: Ablation study on two training methods.

k), and when the 'Multi-path' is removed, the translation quality decreases by 0.76 BLEU (average on all k). This shows that two training methods can both effectively improve the translation quality under low latency, especially 'Future-guided'.

6 Related Work

Previous ST methods are mainly divided into precise read / write policy and stronger predictive ability.

For read / write policy, early policies used segmented translation, and applied full sentence translation to each segment (Bangalore et al., 2012; Cho and Esipova, 2016; Siahbani et al., 2018). Gu et al. (2017) trained an agent through reinforcement learning to decide read / write. Dalvi et al. (2018) proposed STATIC-RW, which first performing S's READs, then alternately performing RW's WRITEs and READs. Ma et al. (2019) proposed wait-k policy, wherein first reads k tokens and then begin synchronizing write and read. Wait-k policy has achieved remarkable performance because it is easy to train and stable, and is widely used in simultaneous translation. Zheng et al. (2019a) generated the gold read / write sequence of input sentence by rules, and then trained an agent with the input sentences and gold read / write sequence. Zheng et al. (2019b) introduces a "delay" token $\{\varepsilon\}$ into the target vocabulary to read one more token. Arivazhagan et al. (2019) proposed MILK, which uses a Bernoulli distribution variable to determine whether to output. Ma et al. (2020) proposed MMA, the implementation of MILK based on Transformer. Zheng et al. (2020) proposed a decoding policy that uses multiple fixed models to accomplish adaptive decoding. Zhang et al. (2020a) propose a novel adaptive segmentation policy for ST.

For predicting future, Matsubara et al. (2000) applied pattern recognition to predict verbs in advance. Grissom II et al. (2014) used a Markov chain to predict the next word and final verb. (Oda et al., 2015) predict unseen syntactic constituents to help generate complete parse trees and perform syntax-based simultaneous translation. Alinejad et al. (2018) added a Predict operation to the agent based on Gu et al. (2017), predicting the next word as an additional input. Elbayad et al. (2020) enhances the wait-k policy by sampling different k to train. Zhang et al. (2020b) proposed future-guided training, which introduces a full-sentence Transformer as the teacher of the ST model and uses future information to guide training through knowledge distillation.

Although the previous methods performed well, they were all evaluated on the traditional MT corpus instead of the real streaming spoken language corpus. Therefore, the previous methods all ignore the robustness and domain adaptation of the ST model in the face of real streaming input. Our method bridges the gap between the MT corpus and the streaming spoken language domain input, and is more robust and adaptable to the spoken language domain.

7 Conclusion and Future Work

Our submitted system won the first place in AutoSimTrans 2021, which is described in this paper. For streaming transcription input from the real scenarios, our proposed char-level wait-k policy is more robust than standard subword-level wait-k. Besides, we also propose two data processing operations to improve the spoken language domain adaptability. For training, we combine two existing training methods that have been proven effective. The experiment on the data provided by the organizer proves the superiority of our method, especially at low latency.

In this competition, we implemented the char-level wait-k policy on the Chinese source. For some language pairs with a large length ratio between the source (char) and the target (bpe), we can read multiple characters at each step to prevent the issue caused by the excessively long char-level source. We put the char-level simultaneous translation on other languages (such as German and English) for both fixed and adaptive policy into our future work.

Acknowledgements

We thank all the anonymous reviewers for their insightful and valuable comments.

References

Ashkan Alinejad, Maryam Siahbani, and Anoop Sarkar. 2018. Prediction improves simultaneous neural machine translation. In Proceedings of the 2018 Conference on Empirical Methods in Natural Language Processing, pages 3022–3027, Brussels, Belgium. Association for Computational Linguistics.

Naveen Arivazhagan, Colin Cherry, Wolfgang Macherey, Chung-cheng Chiu, Semih Yavuz, Ruoming Pang, Wei Li, and Colin Raffel. 2019. Monotonic Infinite Lookback Attention for Simultaneous Machine Translation. pages 1313–1323.

Srinivas Bangalore, Vivek Kumar Rangarajan Sridhar, Prakash Kolan, Ladan Golipour, and Aura Jimenez. 2012. Real-time incremental speech-to-speech translation of dialogs. In Proceedings of the 2012 Conference of the North American Chapter of the Association for Computational Linguistics: Human Language Technologies, pages 437–445, Montréal, Canada. Association for Computational Linguistics.

Colin Cherry, George Foster, Ankur Bapna, Orhan Firat, and Wolfgang Macherey. 2018. Revisiting Character-Based Neural Machine Translation with Capacity and Compression. In Proceedings of the 2018 Conference on Empirical Methods in Natural Language Processing, pages 4295–4305, Brussels, Belgium. Association for Computational Linguistics.

Kyunghyun Cho and Masha Esipova. 2016. Can neural machine translation do simultaneous translation?

Fahim Dalvi, Nadir Durrani, Hassan Sajjad, and Stephan Vogel. 2018. Incremental decoding and training methods for simultaneous translation in neural machine translation. In Proceedings of the 2018 Conference of the North American Chapter of the Association for Computational Linguistics: Human Language Technologies, Volume 2 (Short Papers), pages 493–499, New Orleans, Louisiana. Association for Computational Linguistics.

Maha Elbayad, Laurent Besacier, and Jakob Verbeek. 2020. Efficient wait-k models for simultaneous machine translation.

Yingqiang Gao, Nikola I. Nikolov, Yuhuang Hu, and Richard H.R. Hahnloser. 2020. Character-Level Translation with Self-attention. In Proceedings of the 58th Annual Meeting of the Association for Computational Linguistics, pages 1591–1604, Online. Association for Computational Linguistics.

Alvin Grissom II, He He, Jordan Boyd-Graber, John Morgan, and Hal Daumé III. 2014. Don't until the final verb wait: Reinforcement learning for simultaneous machine translation. In Proceedings of the 2014 Conference on Empirical Methods in Natural Language Processing (EMNLP), pages 1342–1352, Doha, Qatar. Association for Computational Linguistics.

Jiatao Gu, Graham Neubig, Kyunghyun Cho, and Victor O.K. Li. 2017. Learning to translate in real-time with neural machine translation. In Proceedings of the 15th Conference of the European Chapter of the Association for Computational Linguistics: Volume 1, Long Papers, pages 1053–1062, Valencia, Spain. Association for Computational Linguistics.

Jason Lee, Kyunghyun Cho, and Thomas Hofmann. 2017. Fully Character-Level Neural Machine Translation without Explicit Segmentation. Transactions of the Association for Computational Linguistics, 5:365–378.

Minqin Li, Haodong Cheng, Yuanjie Wang, Sijia Zhang, Liting Wu, and Yuhang Guo. 2020. BIT's system for the AutoSimTrans 2020. In Proceedings of the First Workshop on Automatic Simultaneous Translation, pages 37–44, Seattle, Washington. Association for Computational Linguistics.

Wang Ling, Isabel Trancoso, Chris Dyer, and Alan W. Black. 2015. Character-based Neural Machine Translation. arXiv:1511.04586 [cs]. ArXiv: 1511.04586.

Mingbo Ma, Liang Huang, Hao Xiong, Renjie Zheng, Kaibo Liu, Baigong Zheng, Chuanqiang Zhang, Zhongjun He, Hairong Liu, Xing Li, Hua Wu, and Haifeng Wang. 2019. STACL: Simultaneous translation with implicit anticipation and controllable latency using prefix-to-prefix framework. In Proceedings of the 57th Annual Meeting of the Association for Computational Linguistics, pages 3025–3036, Florence, Italy. Association for Computational Linguistics.

Xutai Ma, Juan Miguel Pino, James Cross, Liezl Puzon, and Jiatao Gu. 2020. Monotonic multihead attention. In International Conference on Learning Representations.

Keiichi Matsubara, Shigeki Iwashima, Nobuo Kawaguchi, Katsuhiko Toyama, and Yasuyoshi Inagaki. 2000. Simultaneous japenese-english interpretation based on early predictoin of english verb. In Proceedings of the 4th Symposium on Natural Languauge Processing(SNLP-2000), pages 268–273.

Nikola I. Nikolov, Yuhuang Hu, Mi Xue Tan, and Richard H.R. Hahnloser. 2018. Character-level Chinese-English Translation through ASCII Encoding. In Proceedings of the Third Conference on Machine Translation: Research Papers, pages 10–16, Brussels, Belgium. Association for Computational Linguistics.

Yusuke Oda, Graham Neubig, Sakriani Sakti, Tomoki Toda, and Satoshi Nakamura. 2015. Syntax-based simultaneous translation through prediction of unseen syntactic constituents. In Proceedings of the 53rd Annual Meeting of the Association for Computational Linguistics and the 7th International Joint Conference on Natural Language Processing (Volume 1: Long Papers), pages 198–207, Beijing, China. Association for Computational Linguistics.

Myle Ott, Sergey Edunov, Alexei Baevski, Angela Fan, Sam Gross, Nathan Ng, David Grangier, and Michael Auli. 2019. fairseq: A fast, extensible toolkit for sequence modeling. In Proceedings of the 2019 Conference of the North American Chapter of the Association for Computational Linguistics (Demonstrations), pages 48–53, Minneapolis, Minnesota. Association for Computational Linguistics.

Kishore Papineni, Salim Roukos, Todd Ward, and Wei-Jing Zhu. 2002. Bleu: a method for automatic evaluation of machine translation. In Proceedings of the 40th Annual Meeting of the Association for Computational Linguistics, pages 311–318, Philadelphia, Pennsylvania, USA. Association for Computational Linguistics.

Peyman Passban, Qun Liu, and Andy Way. 2018. Improving Character-Based Decoding Using Target-Side Morphological Information for Neural Machine Translation. In Proceedings of the 2018 Conference of the North American Chapter of the Association for Computational Linguistics: Human Language Technologies, Volume 1 (Long Papers), pages 58–68, New Orleans, Louisiana. Association for Computational Linguistics.

Danielle Saunders, Weston Feely, and Bill Byrne. 2020. Inference-only sub-character decomposition improves translation of unseen logographic characters. In Proceedings of the 7th Workshop on Asian Translation, pages 170–177, Suzhou, China. Association for Computational Linguistics.

Rico Sennrich. 2017. How Grammatical is Character-level Neural Machine Translation? Assessing MT Quality with Contrastive Translation Pairs. In Proceedings of the 15th Conference of the European Chapter of the Association for Computational Linguistics: Volume 2, Short Papers, pages 376–382, Valencia, Spain. Association for Computational Linguistics.

Rico Sennrich, Barry Haddow, and Alexandra Birch. 2016. Neural machine translation of rare words with subword units. In Proceedings of the 54th Annual Meeting of the Association for Computational Linguistics (Volume 1: Long Papers), pages 1715–1725, Berlin, Germany. Association for Computational Linguistics.

Maryam Siahbani, Hassan Shavarani, Ashkan Alinejad, and Anoop Sarkar. 2018. Simultaneous translation using optimized segmentation. In Proceedings of the 13th Conference of the Association for Machine Translation in the Americas (Volume 1: Research Papers), pages 154–167, Boston, MA. Association for Machine Translation in the Americas.

Gongbo Tang, Rico Sennrich, and Joakim Nivre. 2020. Understanding Pure Character-Based Neural Machine Translation: The Case of Translating Finnish into English. In Proceedings of the 28th International Conference on Computational Linguistics, pages 4251–4262, Barcelona, Spain (Online). International Committee on Computational Linguistics.

Ashish Vaswani, Noam Shazeer, Niki Parmar, Jakob Uszkoreit, Llion Jones, Aidan N Gomez, Ł ukasz Kaiser, and Illia Polosukhin. 2017. Attention is all you need. In I. Guyon, U. V. Luxburg, S. Bengio, H. Wallach, R. Fergus, S. Vishwanathan, and R. Garnett, editors, Advances in Neural Information Processing Systems 30, pages 5998–6008. Curran Associates, Inc.

Zhen Yang, Wei Chen, Feng Wang, and Bo Xu. 2016. A Character-Aware Encoder for Neural Machine Translation. In Proceedings of COLING 2016, the 26th International Conference on Computational Linguistics: Technical Papers, pages 3063–3070, Osaka, Japan. The COLING 2016 Organizing Committee.

Ruiqing Zhang, Xiyang Wang, Chuanqiang Zhang, Zhongjun He, Hua Wu, Zhi Li, Haifeng Wang, Ying Chen, and Qinfei Li. 2021. Bstc: A large-scale chinese-english speech translation dataset. arXiv preprint arXiv:2104.03575.

Ruiqing Zhang, Chuanqiang Zhang, Zhongjun He, Hua Wu, and Haifeng Wang. 2020a. Learning adaptive segmentation policy for simultaneous translation. In Proceedings of the 2020 Conference on Empirical Methods in Natural Language Processing (EMNLP), pages 2280–2289, Online. Association for Computational Linguistics.

Shaolei Zhang, Yang Feng, and Liangyou Li. 2020b. Future-guided incremental transformer for simultaneous translation.

Baigong Zheng, Kaibo Liu, Renjie Zheng, Mingbo Ma, Hairong Liu, and Liang Huang. 2020. Simultaneous translation policies: From fixed to adaptive. In Proceedings of the 58th Annual Meeting of the Association for Computational Linguistics, pages 2847–2853, Online. Association for Computational Linguistics.

Baigong Zheng, Renjie Zheng, Mingbo Ma, and Liang Huang. 2019a. Simpler and faster learning of adaptive policies for simultaneous translation. In Proceedings of the 2019 Conference on Empirical Methods in Natural Language Processing and the 9th International Joint Conference on Natural Language Processing (EMNLP-IJCNLP), pages 1349–1354, Hong Kong, China. Association for Computational Linguistics.

Baigong Zheng, Renjie Zheng, Mingbo Ma, and Liang Huang. 2019b. Simultaneous translation with flexible policy via restricted imitation learning. In Proceedings of the 57th Annual Meeting of the Association for Computational Linguistics, pages 5816–5822, Florence, Italy. Association for Computational Linguistics.

BIT's system for AutoSimTrans 2021

Mengge Liu , **Shuoying Chen** , **Minqin Li** , **Zhipeng Wang** and **Yuhang Guo**[*]
Beijing Institute of Technology, Beijing, China
`lmg864355282@gmail.com` `guoyuhang@bit.edu.cn`

Abstract

In this paper we introduce our Chinese-English simultaneous translation system participating in AutoSimTrans 2021. In simultaneous translation, translation quality and latency are both important. In order to reduce the translation latency, we cut the streaming-input source sentence into segments and translate the segments before the full sentence is received. In order to obtain high-quality translations, we pre-train a translation model with adequate corpus and fine-tune the model with domain adaptation and sentence length adaptation. The experimental results on the development dataset show that our system performs better than the baseline system.

1 Introduction

Machine translation greatly facilitates communication between people of different language, and the current neural machine translation model has achieved great success in machine translation field. However, for some occasions that have higher requirements for translation speed, such as in simultaneous interpretation dynamic subtitles and dynamic subtitles application fields. Machine translation models that use full sentences as translation units need to wait for the speaker to speak the full sentence before starting translation, in which the translation delay is unacceptable. In order to reduce the delay, translation must start before the complete sentence is received. But at the same time the incomplete sentence may have grammatical errors and semantic incompleteness, and the translation quality will decrease compared to the result obtained by full sentences. Further more, different languages may have different word order. There are also many reordering phenomenon when translating between Chinese and English which both belong to the same SVO sentence structure. Sentence reordering and different word-order expression habits bring a great difficult to simultaneous translation.

Since the latency of using a full sentence as translation unit is unacceptable, and the translation of incomplete sentences is difficult and not guaranteed to obtain reliable translations, we consider cutting long sentence into appropriate sub-sentences. And each sub-sentence is grammatically correct and semantically complete to get suitable translation result. By decomposing translating long sentences into translating shorter sub-sentences, the translation can be started before the complete long sentence is received. This strategy of achieving low-latency simultaneous translation can be summarized as segmentation strategy (Rangarajan Sridhar et al., 2013). At the same time, it is observed that a sentence can be divided into independent sub-sentences for translation. For the example in table 1, Chinese and English sentences can be cut, and the Chinese sub-sentences can be translated as a shorter translation unit. According to this example, we can also observe that there is no cross alignment between the two sub-sentences, that is, the English translation of the first Chinese sub-sentence has no semantic and word connections with the translation of second Chinese sub-sentence, and there is no cross word alignment between the two sub-sentences. This phenomenon indicates that it is feasible to divide the full sentence in the parallel corpus into shorter sub-sentences.

In the following of this paper, the second part will introduce the overall framework of the model, the third part will give a detailed description of the fine-tuning, finally will ex-

[*]Corresponding author

Proceedings of the 2nd Workshop on Automatic Simultaneous Translation, pages 12–18
June 10, 2021.

Source sentence	各位	亲爱	的	朋友	们	,	早上好	!
Target sentence	Ladies and gentlemen ,	dear		friend	s	,	good morning	.

Table 1: Segment example, first sub-sentence is in red and the second one is in black.

plain and analysis the experiment results.

2 System Architecture

This part mainly introduces the overall framework of our submission in AutoSimulTrans 2021 competition. The whole model uses typical segmentation strategy to achieve simultaneous translation. It consists of a sentence boundary detector and a machine translation module. The sentence boundary detector reads the streaming input text and obtains the appropriate segments. The segments are input to the downstream translation module, and the translation result of each segment is obtained and then spliced to obtain the full translation. The overall framework of the entire model is shown in the figure 1.

2.1 Sentence Boundary Detector

The sentence boundary detector can also be regarded as a text classifier. For the streaming-input sentence, detector needs to be able to judge whether the received part can be used as a suitable segment to be translated. The specific implementation of the boundary detector is based on a pre-trained Chinese BERT(Devlin et al. (2018)) model as a text representation, add a fully connected layer to form a classifier. In terms of data, long sentences are divided into segments according to punctuation marks, segments are regarded as sub-sentences. Positive and negative examples are constructed according to such rules to fine-tune the pre-trained model to obtain a classifier achieving an accuracy of 92.5%. According to the above processes, a boundary detector that can process streaming input text is constructed.

2.2 Translation Module

The translation module is implemented with the tensor2tensor framework, training the transformer-big model(Vaswani et al., 2017) as a machine translation module. We use the pre-training and fine-tuning method to get better performance on the target task.

First, we use the CWMT19 data set as a large-scale corpus to pre-train machine translation model. The CWMT19 corpus is a standard Chinese and English text corpus, but the target test set in the competition is the speech transcription and translation results, which have domain difference with the standard text. So it is necessary to use speech domain corpus to fine-tune the translation model. On the other hand, the translator needs to translate the sub-sentences when decoding. There is a mismatch between the length and the amount of information between the sub-sentence and the longer full sentences. So we further fine-tune the translation model to make it adapted to sub-sentences translation.

3 Fine-tuning Corpus

3.1 Domain fine-tuning

In order to make the machine translation model trained on the standard text corpus more suitable for translating the transcriptions in the speech field, the translation model needs to be fine-tuned with the corpus of the corresponding speech field. We use the manual transcription and translation text of the Chinese speech provided by the organizer as parallel corpus to fine-tune the pre-training translation model.

3.2 Sentence length fine-tuning

The pre-training and domain fine-tuning processes only train the translation model on the full sentence corpus. But when the model is used to perform the simultaneous translation and decoding process, the sub-sentences are needed to be translated, which causes mismatch between training and testing. In order to make the machine translation model adapt to the shorter sub-sentences translation sence, it is necessary to construct a sub-sentence corpus composed of Chinese and English sub-sentence pairs to further fine-tune the machine translation model. In order to meet the requirements of domain adaptation at the same time, sub-sentence corpus is constructed based

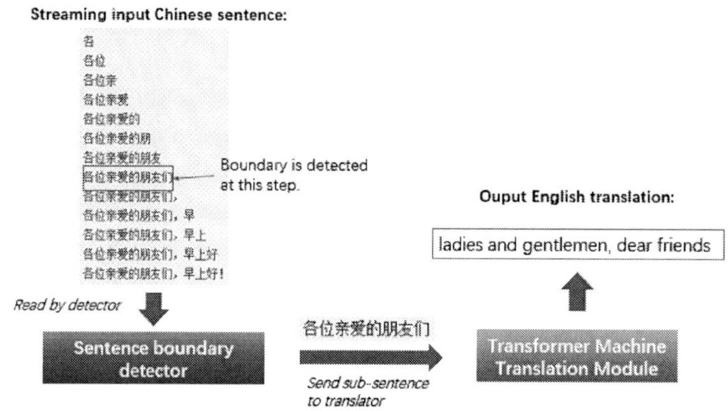

Figure 1: System Architecture

on the Chinese-English corpus provided by the organizer to fine-tune the machine translation model to adapt to the sub-sentence translation scenario. The following is a detailed description of the specific method of processing the full sentence into a sub-sentences.

The ideal sentence segmentation effect is that if the Chinese and English sentence pairs are divided into two or more sub-sentence pairs, Chinese sentence and the English sentence should be cut at the same time to obtain the same number of sub-sentences, and corresponding Chinese and English sub-sentences should contain same information. In another word, using Chinese sub-sentence can get enough information to translate the corresponding English sub-sentence. In order to meet the requirements of information integrity, we use the word alignment tool to obtain the word alignment information between Chinese and English sentence pairs, using the *fast_align*(Dyer et al., 2013) word alignment tool to obtain Chinese to English and English to Chinese alignments respectively, and merge them into symmetry alignments. The result of word alignment, such as the Chinese input sentence $X = \{x_1, x_2, ..., x_n\}$ and the target English sentence $Y = \{y_1, y_2, ..., y_m\}$, we can get a set of alignment results $A = \{< x_i, y_j > | x_i \in X, y_j \in Y\}$.

Then, the word alignment matrix is obtained according to the word alignment results. The segmentation of the Chinese and English full-sentence pairs is equivalent to the division of the word alignment matrix. The word alignment matrix can be divided into four blocks according to a division position, when the lower left and upper right matrices are both zero matrices, meaning that two sub-sentences do not have cross-word alignment. And sub-sentences can be obtained at the current segmentation position. Moreover, the traversal-based division algorithm can divide a sentence with multiple suitable methods, effectively increasing the number of sub-sentence pairs in the sub-sentence corpus.

An example of sentence segmentation using word alignment matrix is shown in the figure 2. According to the alignment results of Chinese and English words, an alignment matrix is constructed. The position is '1' means the Chinese word and English word have alignment and the remaining position have no alignment. Two dashed boxes are identified in the figure, corresponding to two reasonable division results. The dashed box is the first sub-sentence and remain part is second sub-sentence. We retain all reasonable fragmentation results when segmenting sentences, that is, both segmentation results in the figure will be retained.

4 Experiment

4.1 Experiment settings

The boundary detector is based on the pretraining BERT of *chinese_L-12_H-768_A-12* as the pre-training model, the hidden size of fully connected layer is the same of BERT. Using the simultaneous interpretation corpus provided by the organizer, cutting into sub-

	各位	亲爱	的	朋友	们	,	早上好	!
ladies		1						
and			1					
gentlemen	1	1						
,			1					
dear		1						
friend				1	1			
,					1	1		
good							1	
morning							1	
!								1

Figure 2: Segment sentence by word alignment matrix.

sentences based on punctuation, constructing positive and negative examples for fine-tuning training. Then we obtain a sentence boundary recognizer that can recognize sentence boundaries and realize real-time segmentation of streaming input.

Our translation model is based on the *tensor2tensor* framework. We set the parameters of the model as *transformer_big*. And we set the parameter problem as *translate_enzh_wmt32k_rev*. We train the model on 6 GPUs for 9 days.

In experiment, we pre-train translator on CWMT19 dataset, fine-tune translator on BSTC(Zhang et al., 2021) dataset, and evaluate model on BSTC development dataset containing transcription and translation of 16 speeches. CWMT19 is a standard text translation corpus. BSTC contains 68h Chinese speech and corresponding Chinese transcription and English translation text. In this article, we only use Chinese and English texts in the speech field.

4.2 Sub-sentence fine-tuning

In terms of domain adaptability, we use golden transcribed text as fine-tuning corpus. In terms of sentence length adaptability, we use corpus containing only golden transcriptions and corpus containing ASR and golden transcriptions to construct sub-sentence corpus, and use boundary detector as a filter to remove some unsuitable sub-sentence. The situation of fine-tuning corpus is shown in the table 2. The same sentence boundary detector is used by all model, and different machine translation modules are as follows:

- domain fine-tuned: pre-trained on CWMT19 corpus, and fine-tuned on golden transcription.

- sub-sentence fine-tuned(golden+ASR): based on domain fine-tuned model, fine-tuned by segmented golden&ASR transcription corpus.

- sub-sentence fine-tuned(golden): based on domain fine-tuned model, fine-tuned by segmented golden transcription corpus.

- sub-sentence fine-tuned(filtered golden): based on domain fine-tuned model, fine-tuned by filtered segmented golden transcription corpus.

Learning rate is set as 2e-5 in fine-tuning, domain fine-tuning is carried out for 2000 steps and segmentation fine-tuning is carried out for 4000 steps.

4.3 Latency metric

Here is the definition of AL latency metric as used in (Ma et al., 2018). t is decoding step, τ is cut-off decoding step where source sentence is finished, $g(t)$ denote the number of source words read by encoder at decoding step t, and $r = |x|/|y|$ is target-to-source length ratio. The lower AL value means lower latency and better real-time simultaneous system.

$$AL = \frac{1}{\tau}\sum_{t=1}^{\tau} g(t) - \frac{t-1}{\gamma}$$

$$\tau = \arg\min_{t}[g(t) = |x|]$$

4.4 Results and analysis

The performance of each model on the development set is list in table 3.According to the

Fine-tuning corpus	Type	Sentence Pairs
golden transcription	full-sentence	37k
segmented golden&ASR transcription	sub-sentence	2555k
segmented golden transcription	sub-sentence	668k
segmented golden(filtered) transcription	sub-sentence	246k

Table 2: First full-sentence corpus is provided by organizer. Three sub-sentence corpus constructed by word alignment, constructed from golden and ASR transcription corpus provided by organizer. The third line is the filtered segmentation corpus.

experimental results, the performance of the fine-tuning model did not meet expectations. Using only the corpus made by golden transcription corpus brought a greater quality reduction compared to using corpus including the ASR and golden transcriptions. Comparing with models fine-tuned by golden transcription and model fine-tuned by filtered golden transcription, we can find that although the number of sentences in sub-sentences corpus has decreased after filtering, it has obtained a relatively high score, which reflects the effectiveness of the filtering operation.

The main reason for the unsatisfactory fine-tuning effect may because the sub-sentence corpus contains too much noise. It may be difficult to obtain high-quality segmentation results by the word alignment results. Although we have filtered many inappropriate sentences, there is still a lot of noise in the sub-sentence corpus. And because the sub-sentences are shorter, the translation errors of the sentence pair in fine-tuning corpus will have a greater negative impacts on translation model.

Here is an example to explain the difficulty of sentence division. In the sentence showed in table 4, we list the source sentence and target sentence, and also direct translation for each phrase just for understanding the meaning of Chinese words. From the perspective of word alignment, it can be easily divided from the comma position to obtain two sub-sentences. For the first sub-sentence pair, the Chinese and English sub-sentences contain same information, and good English translation results can be easily obtained according to Chinese. But for the second sub-sentence pair, it's hard to obtain golden translation relay only on Chinese sub-sentence. If you directly translate the Chinese, you may get a translation result similar to "amazing by hearing. ". This is because the result of golden translation is obtained with full sentence, and in order to make the translated English expression more fluent, free translation is carried out. If the translation model only reads the second sub-sentence, it is difficult to obtain a suitable translation result relative to the golden result.

5 Related work

This article uses segmentation strategy to achieve low-latency simultaneous translation. There are also some similar works use segmentation strategy to divide long sentences into segments for translation, (Xiong et al., 2019) focus on improving the coherence of the sub-sentences translation results, (Zhang et al., 2020) focus on solving the problem of long-distance reordering in simultaneous translation.

In addition, there are two different strategies for achieving simultaneous translation: one is a more flexible translation strategy based on sentence prefixes. The process of simultaneous translation is defined as a read-write action sequence from the perspective of behavior. It is necessary to define a suitable strategy to find out the action sequence, and adjust the translator to make the model more suitable for the translation of sentence prefixes (Ma et al., 2018)(Arivazhagan et al., 2019). Another type is translation based on dynamic refresh without the need to adjust the machine translation model. Whenever the input increases, translate all input and overwrite the translation result that has been generated last time (Niehues et al., 2016)(Arivazhagan et al., 2020b)(Arivazhagan et al., 2020a).

6 Conclusion

In this paper we describe a simultaneous translation method that reduces translation

Model	AL	BLEU
domain fine-tuned	7.467	19.45
sub-sentence fine-tuned(golden+ASR)	7.478	19.02
sub-sentence fine-tuned(golden)	7.823	16.28
sub-sentence fine-tuned(filtered golden)	7.795	16.67

Table 3: Performance of each model on the development set. AL is latency metric and BLEU is text quality metric.

Source sentence	这些东西	都是	大自然奇特的物产	,	听听都很奇特。
Literal translation	These things	are all	nature's amazing creations	,	amazing by hearing.
Target sentence	These	are all	amazing creations of the nature	,	you can tell just from their names .

Table 4: A example hard to segment. The sentence can be segmented by comma. The literal translation of second sub-sentence is quite different from the target.

delay by cutting the full sentence into sub-sentences.We fine-tune a pre-trained translation model in terms of domain and sentence length. The sub-sentence corpus is constructed by word alignment, we found that directly using all the sub-sentences we obtained has a negative impact on translation performance, but it can be improved after filtering. In the end, we obtained translation results that exceeded the baseline model.

Acknowledgements

Supported by the National Key Research and Development Program of China (No. 2016YFB0801200)

References

Naveen Arivazhagan, Colin Cherry, Wolfgang Macherey, Chung-Cheng Chiu, Semih Yavuz, Ruoming Pang, Wei Li, and Colin Raffel. 2019. Monotonic infinite lookback attention for simultaneous machine translation. *arXiv preprint arXiv:1906.05218*.

Naveen Arivazhagan, Colin Cherry, Wolfgang Macherey, and George Foster. 2020a. Re-translation versus streaming for simultaneous translation. *arXiv preprint arXiv:2004.03643*.

Naveen Arivazhagan, Colin Cherry, Isabelle Te, Wolfgang Macherey, Pallavi Baljekar, and George Foster. 2020b. Re-translation strategies for long form, simultaneous, spoken language translation. In *ICASSP 2020-2020 IEEE International Conference on Acoustics, Speech and Signal Processing (ICASSP)*, pages 7919–7923. IEEE.

Jacob Devlin, Ming-Wei Chang, Kenton Lee, and Kristina Toutanova. 2018. Bert: Pre-training of deep bidirectional transformers for language understanding. *arXiv preprint arXiv:1810.04805*.

Chris Dyer, Victor Chahuneau, and Noah A. Smith. 2013. A simple, fast, and effective reparameterization of IBM model 2. In *Proceedings of the 2013 Conference of the North American Chapter of the Association for Computational Linguistics: Human Language Technologies*, pages 644–648, Atlanta, Georgia. Association for Computational Linguistics.

Mingbo Ma, Liang Huang, Hao Xiong, Renjie Zheng, Kaibo Liu, Baigong Zheng, Chuanqiang Zhang, Zhongjun He, Hairong Liu, Xing Li, et al. 2018. Stacl: Simultaneous translation with implicit anticipation and controllable latency using prefix-to-prefix framework. *arXiv preprint arXiv:1810.08398*.

Jan Niehues, Thai Son Nguyen, Eunah Cho, Thanh-Le Ha, Kevin Kilgour, Markus Müller, Matthias Sperber, Sebastian Stüker, and Alex Waibel. 2016. Dynamic transcription for low-latency speech translation. In *Interspeech*, pages 2513–2517.

Vivek Kumar Rangarajan Sridhar, John Chen, Srinivas Bangalore, Andrej Ljolje, and Rathinavelu Chengalvarayan. 2013. Segmentation strategies for streaming speech translation. In *Proceedings of the 2013 Conference of the North American Chapter of the Association for Computational Linguistics: Human Language Technologies*, pages 230–238, Atlanta, Georgia. Association for Computational Linguistics.

Ashish Vaswani, Noam Shazeer, Niki Parmar, Jakob Uszkoreit, Llion Jones, Aidan N Gomez, Lukasz Kaiser, and Illia Polosukhin. 2017. Attention is all you need. *arXiv preprint arXiv:1706.03762*.

Hao Xiong, Ruiqing Zhang, Chuanqiang Zhang, Zhongjun He, Hua Wu, and Haifeng Wang.

2019. Dutongchuan: Context-aware translation model for simultaneous interpreting. *arXiv preprint arXiv:1907.12984*.

Ruiqing Zhang, Xiyang Wang, Chuanqiang Zhang, Zhongjun He, Hua Wu, Zhi Li, Haifeng Wang, Ying Chen, and Qinfei Li. 2021. Bstc: A large-scale chinese-english speech translation dataset. *arXiv preprint arXiv:2104.03575*.

Ruiqing Zhang, Chuanqiang Zhang, Zhongjun He, Hua Wu, and Haifeng Wang. 2020. Learning adaptive segmentation policy for simultaneous translation. In *Proceedings of the 2020 Conference on Empirical Methods in Natural Language Processing (EMNLP)*, pages 2280–2289.

A Development results

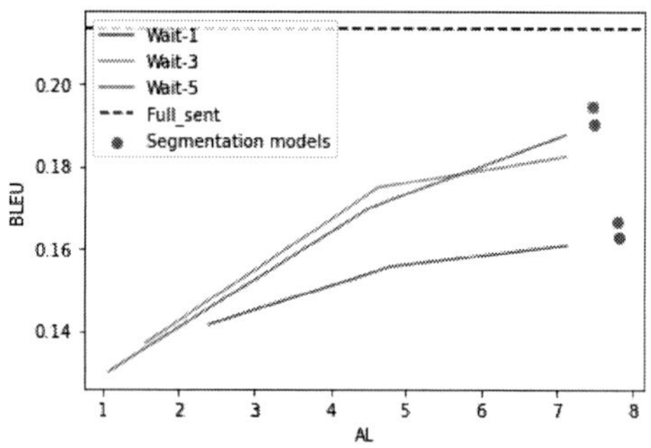

Figure 3: Development results

The results of each model on the development set are shown in the figure 3, where each curve of wait-1, wait-3, wait-5 and full-sent is the wait-k series model and full-sentence model provided by the organizer. Each model is a transformer neural machine translation model. Each scattered point represents a segmentation model in this article. According to the results, it can be seen that the domain fine-tuning model and a better-performed sub-sentence fine-tuning model are better than the wait-k series model.

XMU's Simultaneous Translation System at NAACL 2021

Shuangtao Li[1] and **Jinming Hu**[1]
and **Boli Wang**[2] and **Xiaodong Shi**[3*] and **Yidong Chen**[3]
School of Informatics, Xiamen University / Xiamen, China
[1]{lishuangtao,todtom@stu.xmu.edu.com}
[2]me@bo-li.wang
[3]{mandel,ydchen}@xmu.edu.cn

Abstract

This paper describes XMU's two systems submitted to the simultaneous translation evaluation at the 2nd automatic simultaneous translation workshop, which are for Zh->En text-to-text translation and Zh->En speech-to-text translation. In both systems, our translation model is based on Transformer. To translate streaming text, we use an adaptive policy to split the text into appropriate segments and translate them monotonically. Our speech-to-text system is a pipeline system, in which the MT component is exactly the same as our text-to-text system.

1 Introduction

Simultaneous translation refers to translating the message from the speaker to the audience in real-time without interrupting the speaker. It is widely used in many scenarios such as international conferences and business negotiations. Simultaneous machine translation is a challenging task and has become an increasingly popular research field in recent years.

There have been some researches on simultaneous translation of speech input (Niehues et al., 2018; Ma et al., 2020b,c; Ren et al., 2020), and some researches focused on text translation (Arivazhagan et al., 2019; Zhang et al., 2020; Ma et al., 2020a).

In this paper, we describe our two systems submitted to the simultaneous translation evaluation at the 2nd automatic simultaneous translation workshop, which are for Zh->En text-to-text translation and Zh->En speech-to-text translation. We build our systems with the state-of-the-art method (Zhang et al., 2020), and verify the effectiveness of this method.

2 Text-to-text Track

In this section, we describe our system submitted to Zh->En text-to-text simultaneous translation track.

The main idea of this system is how human interpreters work. While listening to speakers, human interpreters constantly translate text segments that are appropriate to translate without waiting for more words, and meanwhile making the translation grammatically tolerable. Text segments considered appropriate to translate usually have clear and definite meaning, because the translation of such a segment is not likely to be changed by subsequent text. The authors of Zhang et al. (2020) refered to such segments Meaningful Units (MU) and gived MUs a precise difinition. See Table 1 for an illustration.

Our system works like a human interpreter described above and is composed of an MU classification model and a machine translation model. Once a segment is classified to be an MU by the MU classifier, the MT model uses forced decoding with previous translation as the prefix to translate the segment, as shown in Table 1.

2.1 Machine translation

Our machine translation model is implemented with FAIRSEQ[1] (Ott et al., 2019).

Data and preprocessing. The data we use are CWMT19[2] (9.1M parallel sentences pairs) and the simultaneous translation corpus (39K parallel sentences pairs) provided by the organizer of the workshop.

We do the following steps to preprocess the data.

- Filtering. The sentence pairs whose English sentence is longer than 120 words are filtered out.

* Corresponding author.

[1] https://github.com/pytorch/fairseq

[2] http://mteval.cipsc.org.cn:81/agreement/description

Proceedings of the 2nd Workshop on Automatic Simultaneous Translation, pages 19–23
June 10, 2021.

Source:	牛顿	||	发现	了	||	牛顿	运动	定律
	Newton		discover	tense particle		Newton	motion	law
Simul. Interpretation:	Newton	||		discovered	||			Newton' s laws of motion

Table 1: An illustration of how a human interpreter work. The source sentence is splited to three MUs (separated by "||"), and an interpreter translates the MUs in order and makes them form a grammatically correct sentence.

- There are a few punctuation marks, numbers and letters in the data which are in full width. They are converted to half width characters.

- There are a few Chinese characters in the data which are traditional characters. They are converted to simplified ones.

- Chinese segmentation. All Chinese sentences are segmented with Jieba Chinese Segmentation Tool[3].

- English tokenization. All English sentences are tokenized and truecased with Moses[4].

- Byte-pair-encoding (BPE) (Sennrich et al., 2016). Both Chinese and English data are encoded by BPE with Subword-NMT[5]. The number of merge operations for each language is set to 30K.

Modeling and training. Our translation model's architecture is base Transformer (Vaswani et al., 2017). We use Adam optimizer (Kingma and Ba, 2015) to optimize the loss. We use weight decay of $1e^{-4}$ and dropout with probability of 0.2 for regularization. Label smoothing with ϵ of 0.1 is applied to our model. During inference, we set beam size to 20.

Our model is first pretrained on CWMT and then finetuned on the the training set of the Baidu Speech Translation Corpus (Zhang et al., 2021). We set learning rate to $5e^{-4}$ in the pretraining stage and $3e^{-5}$ in the fine-tuning stage. The learning rate is linearly increased for the first 4000 training steps, and is decreased following an inverse squareroot schedule.

2.2 MU classifier

Modeling and training. The MU classifier is a binary classifier. Given a source word sequence $x = \{x_1, x_2, ..., x_n\}$, the MU classifier determines whether x ends with an MU, and if so the MT will translate x with forced decoding. The input of the classifier is x and m "future" words $x_f = \{x_{n+1}, x_{n+2}, ..., x_{n+m}\}$, where m is a hyperparameter. The outputs are the probabilities of two classes $p(c = 1)$ and $p(c = 0)$, which mean x ends with an MU or not. x will be classified into class 1 if $p(c = 1) > t$, where t is a threshold set based on experience. Obviously, we can control the latency of simultaneous translation by modifying m. Later in experiments, it will be shown that we can also control the latency by modifying t. In our system, m is always set to 2.

x	$x_f(m = 2)$	c
牛顿 ||	发现 了	1
牛顿 || 发现	了 牛顿	0
牛顿 || 发现 了 ||	牛顿 运动	1
牛顿 || 发现 了 || 牛顿	运动 定律	0

Table 2: MU samples for the MU classifier. "||" is a symbol to separate MUs. $c = 1$ means that x ends with an MU, otherwise not.

The MU classifier is based on a chinese BERT (Devlin et al., 2019)[6]. We use the base model and fine-tune it with a learning rate of $5e^{-4}$.

Generating MU samples. To build an MU classifier, we need to generate MU samples just like the samples in Table 2. For each sentence of length N, we generate $N - m$ examples for it, and every MU sample is a triple $< x, x_f, c >$. When we generate examples, c is set to 1 if x ends with an MU, else it is set to 0. In our system, we generate MU samples for every sentence pairs in CWMT and the simultaneous translation corpus. Our MU samples are a little different from the MU samples in Zhang et al. (2020). In their work, the future words of a sample can be less than m, but not in this paper. We do not need training samples whose future words are less than m, because during inference when the future words are less than m, the sentence is already a whole sentence and thus can be fed into MT.

We use the *basic method* proposed in Zhang et al. (2020) to generate MU samples.

[3]https://github.com/fxsjy/jieba

[4]https://github.com/moses-smt/mosesdecoder

[5]https://github.com/rsennrich/subword-nmt

[6]https://github.com/649453932/Bert-Chinese-Text-Classification-Pytorch

3 Speech-to-text Track

In this section, we describe our system submitted to Zh->En speech-to-text simultaneous translation track.

This system is a pipeline of three stages: (1) speech recognition, (2) punctuation restoration, and (3) streaming machine translation. The third stage is exactly the same as the system described in Section 2. In other words, the system described in Section 2 is a part of our speech-to-text system, and therefore it will not be repeated in this section. This section only describes the stage (1) and stage (2).

3.1 Speech recognition

Instead of building a speech recognition model, we use Baidu's real time speech recognition service[7]. In our system, We call the API of this service to recognize streaming speech. It is important to note that although the ASR does not output punctuation, it separates different sentences, that is, the ASR outputs are many segmented sentences instead of one sentence.

3.2 Punctuation restoration

The recognition results of Baidu's asr service do not have punctuation, but the input of our MT model needs punctuation. As a result we build a model to restore the punctuation for every recognition result. We use a BERT-based (Devlin et al., 2019) sequence labeling model (Chen and Shi, 2020) to do punctuation restoration. This model labels every Chinese character in a sentence, and for the model we only consider four classes: comma, period, question mark and no punctuation.

4 Experiments

In this section, we evaluate our two systems on the development set of the Baidu Speech Translation Corpus (Zhang et al., 2021). The two used metrics are case-sensitive detokenized BLEU (Papineni et al., 2002) and Consecutive Wait (CW) (Neubig et al., 2017), for translation quality and latency respectively. CW considers on how many source words are waited for consecutively between two target words, and thus larger CW means longer latency. We use SacreBLEU (Post, 2018)to compute BLEU scores.

[7]https://cloud.baidu.com/doc/SPEECH/s/2k5dllqxj

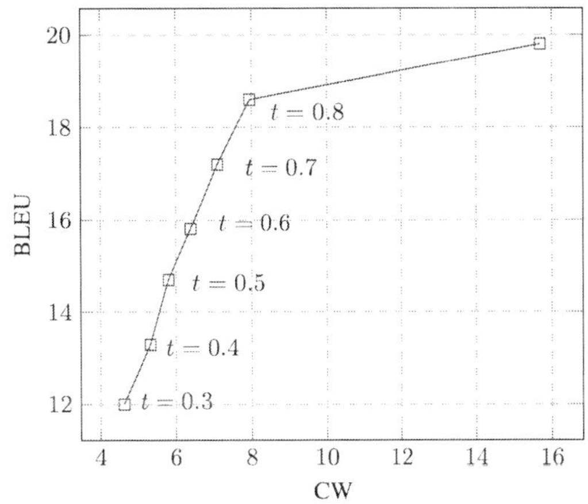

Figure 1: Translation quality against latency of different thresholds t. The rightmost point is not a result of simultaneous translation, but a result got by translating complete sentences.

4.1 Text-to-text track

We set the threshold t in the MU classifier to various values and get multiple results, as shown in Figure 1. It is worth noting that the rightmost point in Figure 1 is not a result of simultaneous translation. This result is got by translating every sentence after it is finished, i.e., we get this result by translating whole sentences.

4.2 Speech-to-text track

The experimental results are shown in Figure 2. Similarly, the rightmost point is not a result of simultaneous translation. Because the speech in the development set is difficult for ASR, the ASR does not perform well, resulting in a character error rate of 35.3%. The errors caused by ASR are brought to MT, and thus the BLEU is much lower than in the text-to-text track.

4.3 Analysis

From Figure 1 and Figure 2, we can observe that the larger the threshold t is, the longer the latency is. This is because the larger the threshold t is, the longer the detected MUs are, which further leads to longer waiting time between two translations. We can also observe that the larger the threshold t is, the higher the translation quality is. This is because the larger the threshold t is, the more likely a detected MU is a true MU and thus the translation of the detected MU will not be changed by subsequent incoming text. Table 3 is an illustration for this.

Source:	好 ， 让 我们 来看 下个 例子 。 okay let we look next example
Reference:	Okay , let 's look at the next example .
Simultaneous Translation ($t = 0.7$):	OK , let 's look at the next example .
Simultaneous Translation ($t = 0.5$):	Okay , || let 's look at the next example .
Simultaneous Translation ($t = 0.3$):	Okay , || let 's do it . || let 's look at the next example .

Table 3: An illustration of text-to-text simultaneous translation with different threshold t. "||" is a symbol for separating the translations of detected MUs.

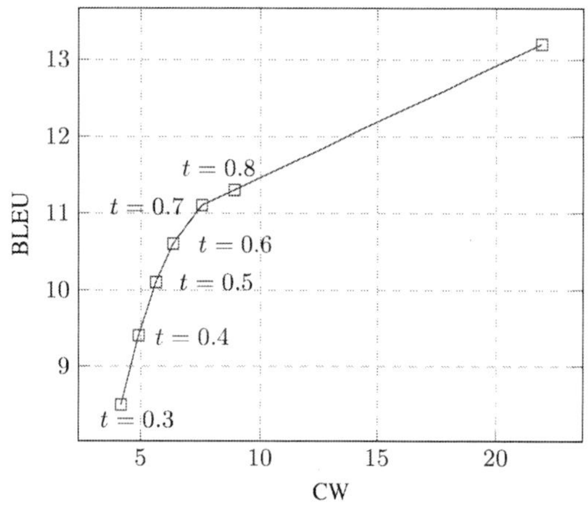

Figure 2: Translation quality against latency of different thresholds t. The rightmost point is not a result of simultaneous translation, but a result got by translating complete sentences.

5 Conclusion

We have built two systems for text-to-text simultaneous translation and speech-to-text simultaneous translation. The key of our systems is the basic adaptive segmentation policy in Zhang et al. (2020). With this policy, simultaneous translation can be achieved without any modification to the MT component, and the latency can be controlled.

In our future work, we would like to study how to improve the cooperation of ASR and MT and the performance of MU classification.

References

N. Arivazhagan, Colin Cherry, Wolfgang Macherey, Chung-Cheng Chiu, Semih Yavuz, R. Pang, Wei Li, and Colin Raffel. 2019. Monotonic infinite lookback attention for simultaneous machine translation. In *ACL*.

Y. Chen and X. Shi. 2020. Improving machine simultaneous interpretation by punctuation recovery. *Journal of Computer Applications*, 40(4):972–977.

J. Devlin, Ming-Wei Chang, Kenton Lee, and Kristina Toutanova. 2019. Bert: Pre-training of deep bidirectional transformers for language understanding. In *NAACL-HLT*.

Diederik P. Kingma and Jimmy Ba. 2015. Adam: A method for stochastic optimization. *CoRR*, abs/1412.6980.

Xutai Ma, J. Pino, James L. Cross, Liezl Puzon, and Jiatao Gu. 2020a. Monotonic multihead attention. *ArXiv*, abs/1909.12406.

Xutai Ma, J. Pino, and Philipp Koehn. 2020b. Simulmt to simulst: Adapting simultaneous text translation to end-to-end simultaneous speech translation. In *AACL/IJCNLP*.

Xutai Ma, Yongqiang Wang, M. Dousti, Philipp Koehn, and J. Pino. 2020c. Streaming simultaneous speech translation with augmented memory transformer. *ArXiv*, abs/2011.00033.

Graham Neubig, Kyunghyun Cho, Jiatao Gu, and Victor O. K. Li. 2017. Learning to translate in real-time with neural machine translation. In *EACL*.

J. Niehues, N. Pham, Thanh-Le Ha, Matthias Sperber, and Alexander H. Waibel. 2018. Low-latency neural speech translation. In *INTERSPEECH*.

Myle Ott, Sergey Edunov, Alexei Baevski, Angela Fan, S. Gross, Nathan Ng, David Grangier, and M. Auli. 2019. fairseq: A fast, extensible toolkit for sequence modeling. In *NAACL-HLT*.

Kishore Papineni, S. Roukos, T. Ward, and Wei-Jing Zhu. 2002. Bleu: a method for automatic evaluation of machine translation. In *ACL*.

Matt Post. 2018. A call for clarity in reporting BLEU scores. In *Proceedings of the Third Conference on Machine Translation: Research Papers*, pages 186–191, Belgium, Brussels. Association for Computational Linguistics.

Yi Ren, J. Liu, Xu Tan, C. Zhang, Tao Qin, Zhou Zhao, and T. Liu. 2020. Simulspeech: End-to-end simultaneous speech to text translation. In *ACL*.

Rico Sennrich, B. Haddow, and Alexandra Birch. 2016. Neural machine translation of rare words with subword units. *ArXiv*, abs/1508.07909.

Ashish Vaswani, Noam Shazeer, Niki Parmar, Jakob Uszkoreit, Llion Jones, Aidan N. Gomez, L. Kaiser, and Illia Polosukhin. 2017. Attention is all you need. *ArXiv*, abs/1706.03762.

Ruiqing Zhang, Xiyang Wang, Chuanqiang Zhang, Zhongjun He, Hua Wu, Zhi Li, Haifeng Wang, Ying Chen, and Qinfei Li. 2021. Bstc: A large-scale chinese-english speech translation dataset. *arXiv preprint arXiv:2104.03575*.

RuiQing Zhang, Chuanqiang Zhang, Zhongjun He, Hua Wu, and Haifeng Wang. 2020. Learning adaptive segmentation policy for simultaneous translation. In *EMNLP*.

System Description on Automatic Simultaneous Translation Workshop

Linjie Chen, Jianzong Wang*, Zhangcheng Huang, Xiongbin Ding, Jing Xiao
Ping An Technology (Shenzhen) Co., Ltd.
chenlinjie887@pingan.com.cn,
jzwang@188.com,
huangzhangcheng624@pingan.com.cn,
dingxiongbin106@pingan.com.cn,
xiaojing661@pingan.com.cn

Abstract

This paper shows our submission on the second automatic simultaneous translation workshop at NAACL2021. We participate in all the two directions of Chinese-to-English translation, Chinese audio→English text and Chinese text→English text. We do data filtering and model training techniques to get the best BLEU score and reduce the average lagging. We propose a two-stage simultaneous translation pipeline system which is composed of Quartznet and BPE-based transformer. We propose a competitive simultaneous translation system and achieves a BLEU score of 24.39 in the audio input track.

1 Introduction

Our submitted system consists of an end to end speech recognition model and a neural machine translation model which follows the traditional pipeline framework in simultaneous translation task. The system input is Chinese audio file and the output is English translation text. A temporary Streaming transcription is obtained by speech recognition model and transmitted into machine translation model to get the target system output.

For automatic speech recognition(ASR) model, we use the QuartzNet model (Kriman et al., 2019) of Nvidia Jarvis. At the moment, we expand the train data set by adding Aishell-1 and data that collected, then using plenty of rules to filter audio data and deal with parallel transcription. Compared to the Jasper model (Li et al., 2019), it can reduce number of parameters quickly by using separable 1D convolutions including time channel.

Our neural machine translation model is Transformer (Vaswani et al., 2017). We use some human rules and the pre-trained language model to filter the parallel corpus. The method of back translation (Sennrich et al., 2016) is also applied to generate synthetic Chinese sentences.

At the step of inference, we apply the wait-k words method (Ma et al., 2018). Both the preprocessing and post-processing are applied to improve the terminology translation and deal with the word error produced by the ASR system.

Since our submission is a two-stage system, the rest of this paper describes separately regards to the Automatic speech recognition(ASR and Machine translation(MT) sub-modules. We firstly describe the training and development datasets we used, then the data filtering methods we applied is introduced. Secondly, the system architecture is discussed and it is verified by the experiments. Lastly, we draw a conclusion of our system by analyzing the experiments.

2 Datasets

For audio data of ASR, we use qianyan audio datasets provided by NAACL workshop (Zhang et al., 2021), Aishell-1 (Hui Bu, 2017) and lip sentences we collect by smartphone(16kHz, 16-bit).

2.1 Audio Data

We invite 20 volunteers in data collection. Each volunteer performed two hours of Mandarin Chinese audio about 1000 sentences in the quiet room. To keep data diversity, different domains of audios were collected, including artificial intelligent, industrial production, business conversation and medical. Finally, we get a total of 19800 sentences (audio and transcription) in this way.

For qianyan audio datasets, we split each audio into sentences according to the sentence-level transcription. After processing, the blank part of all entire audio files was removed, and duration time of audios was reduced from the original 68 hours to about 52 hours.

For AIshell-1 datasets, we firstly deal with transcription files by using rules to get path and filename of every transcription. Then using wave library to read audio files to get the duration time of

Proceedings of the 2nd Workshop on Automatic Simultaneous Translation, pages 24–27
June 10, 2021. ©2021 Association for Computational Linguistics

each audio.

Noting that the audio data and the transcription may not exactly match. In order to improve the accuracy of the data, we use a pre-trained ASR model to transcript audio data to produce text result. Then using similarity matching algorithm to filter audio and original transcription data of lower similarity. Table1 shows the number of train data after filtering.

Table 1: ZH-EN audio train datasets

Data Source	Duration	Total Samples
Qianyan(NAACL)	70hours	36,140
Aishell-1	178hours	120,098
Collection	40hours	19,800

2.2 Text Data

The corpus we use to build our machine translation system is CWMT 19 corpus [1]. It includes both the bilingual and monolingual data.

For the bilingual data, we apply data filtering techniques. The main process is described as follows. Firstly, we set the punctuation ratio and sentence length ratio of the sentence pairs to abandon the sentences higher than the ratio. Secondly, we calculate the cross entropy of each English sentence by a pre-trained language model and removed the sentence pair exceed the threshold. Thirdly, we construct a terminology table using the methods of name entity resolution and word alignment. The terminology such as companies, organizations and human names are replaced with specific words.

For the monolingual data, we follow the method proposed by (Sennrich et al., 2016). We firstly train an English to Chinese machine translation model. Then the monolingual English sentences are translated to generate synthetic Chinese translation. All the synthetic parallel data are filtered with the same strategies applied in bilingual data.

After the filtering process, we normalize the punctuation for both Chinese and English sentences. We apply Chinese word segmentation using LAC toolkit[2] (Jiao et al., 2018) for Chinese sentences. For the English sentences, we apply the Tokenizer and Truecaser toolkit provided by Moses scripts (Koehn et al., 2007). Finally, we train a bytes pairs encoding model and applied it for both Chinese and English sentences.

[1] http://mteval.cipsc.org.cn:81/agreement/AutoSimTrans

[2] https://github.com/baidu/lac

3 System description

The model training process for both the speech recognition and machine translation model are implemented on a device with eight GPUs of Nvidia TESLA V100.

3.1 Automatic speech recognition

The QuartzNet15x5 model is as our based model on ASR, we also use Memory-Self-Attention(MSA) (Luo et al., 2021) modules in the model structure of CTC and RNN-T.

3.1.1 Training Scheme

After data pre-processing, we use the file of json structure to train quartznet 15x5 model. We list the model configuration and train parameters in Table2. When the model was trained, the size of each sample audio should be controlled to less than 16.7 s. To do this, it can improve the accuracy of model and accelerate the training speed. The ASR model was trained over three days and reached to the best WER. After the loss value converged, we use the last saved model to try to transform test datasets and get average score. We use WER-BEAT (Sheshadri et al., 2021) to evaluate our model. And we get closed to 1.0 WER.

Table 2: Model Configuration

Configuration	Value
Sample rate	16,000
Repeat	5
n fft	512
activation	relu
Chinese Vocabulary size	5,270
Optimizer	Adam
residual	true
filters	256/512
batch size	64

To increase the accuracy of model recognition, we use MSA modules in the model structure of CTC and RNN-T. The operation complexity of the model maintains a linear relationship with the length of the input speech, which greatly improves the efficiency of the model, and there will be no serious decline in efficiency as the input increases.

3.1.2 Model Usage

Before we use the model, in order to improve the accuracy of recognition, we need to process the input voice file.

In the end, we only submit one point in the competition. This point is to directly use the previously segmented audio transcription text as the input of the translation model, thereby obtaining a more accurate English text output.

3.2 Machine translation

We use Transformer as our based model on machine translation, the attention mechanism is strength-able at capturing the Semantic relationship on a sentence. The development toolkit we used in machine translation is Marian (Junczys-Dowmunt et al., 2018).

3.2.1 Training Scheme

After completing the data preprocessing on both the bilingual data and back-translated data, we train our baseline model by evaluating BLEU. The language tool for evaluation is uncased 4-gram BLEU (Papineni et al., 2002). We list the model configuration in Table3 and training parameters in Table 4.

We train the model for over three days, the BLEU score increased rapidly at the beginning and the growth slowed after 30 hours. After the loss converged, we collect the last 20 checkpoints of the model in the time interval of one hour and applied checkpoint average to get the final model.

Table 3: Model Configuration

Configuration	Value
Encoder/Decoder depth	6
Attention heads	16
Word Embedding	1024
FFN size	4096
Chinese Vocabulary size	50,000
English Vocabulary size	50,000
Optimizer	Adam

Table 4: Training Parameters

Parameter	Value
Label smoothing	0.1
Learning rate	16
Warmup rates	15,000
Maximum sentence length	120
Clip normalization	5

3.2.2 Fine-tuning

We implement fine-tuning on the Transformer model using the development set of qianyan audio datasets (956 sentence pairs) to improve the translation quality on simultaneous translation task. Since fine-tuning is effective to build a domain-adaptive model.

4 Conclusion

This paper describes our submission to the second automatic simultaneous translation workshop at NAACL2021. We detail our process of data filtering and model training. The Consecutive Wait(CW) (Klein et al., 2017) of the best point reached to 18.4 while we get the BLEU value of 24.39 in the audio input track. In future work, we will continue to research on end-to-end speech translation model from Chinese speech input to English text output.

References

Xingyu Na Bengu Wu Hao Zheng Hui Bu, Jiayu Du. 2017. Aishell-1: An open-source mandarin speech corpus and a speech recognition baseline. In *Oriental COCOSDA 2017*, page Submitted.

Zhenyu Jiao, Shuqi Sun, and Ke Sun. 2018. Chinese lexical analysis with deep bi-gru-crf network. *arXiv preprint arXiv:1807.01882*.

Marcin Junczys-Dowmunt, Roman Grundkiewicz, Tomasz Dwojak, Hieu Hoang, Kenneth Heafield, Tom Neckermann, Frank Seide, Ulrich Germann, Alham Fikri Aji, Nikolay Bogoychev, André F. T. Martins, and Alexandra Birch. 2018. Marian: Fast neural machine translation in C++. In *Proceedings of ACL 2018, Melbourne, Australia, July 15-20, 2018, System Demonstrations*, pages 116–121. Association for Computational Linguistics.

Guillaume Klein, Yoon Kim, Yuntian Deng, Jean Senellart, and Alexander M. Rush. 2017. Opennmt: Open-source toolkit for neural machine translation.

Philipp Koehn, Hieu Hoang, Alexandra Birch, Chris Callison-Burch, Marcello Federico, Nicola Bertoldi, Brooke Cowan, Wade Shen, Christine Moran, Richard Zens, Chris Dyer, Ondrej Bojar, Alexandra Constantin, and Evan Herbst. 2007. Moses: Open source toolkit for statistical machine translation. In *ACL 2007, Proceedings of the 45th Annual Meeting of the Association for Computational Linguistics, June 23-30, 2007, Prague, Czech Republic*. The Association for Computational Linguistics.

Samuel Kriman, Stanislav Beliaev, Boris Ginsburg, Jocelyn Huang, Oleksii Kuchaiev, Vitaly Lavrukhin, Ryan Leary, Jason Li, and Yang Zhang. 2019. Quartznet: Deep automatic speech recognition with 1d time-channel separable convolutions.

Jason Li, Vitaly Lavrukhin, Boris Ginsburg, Ryan Leary, Oleksii Kuchaiev, Jonathan M. Cohen, Huyen

Nguyen, and Ravi Teja Gadde. 2019. Jasper: An end-to-end convolutional neural acoustic model.

Jian Luo, Jianzong Wang, Ning Cheng, and Jing Xiao. 2021. Unidirectional memory-self-attention transducer for online speech recognition.

Mingbo Ma, Liang Huang, Hao Xiong, Kaibo Liu, Chuanqiang Zhang, Zhongjun He, Hairong Liu, Xing Li, and Haifeng Wang. 2018. STACL: simultaneous translation with integrated anticipation and controllable latency. *CoRR*, abs/1810.08398.

Kishore Papineni, Salim Roukos, Todd Ward, and Wei-Jing Zhu. 2002. Bleu: a method for automatic evaluation of machine translation. In *Proceedings of the 40th Annual Meeting of the Association for Computational Linguistics, July 6-12, 2002, Philadelphia, PA, USA*, pages 311–318. ACL.

Rico Sennrich, Barry Haddow, and Alexandra Birch. 2016. Improving neural machine translation models with monolingual data. In *Proceedings of the 54th Annual Meeting of the Association for Computational Linguistics, ACL 2016, August 7-12, 2016, Berlin, Germany, Volume 1: Long Papers*. The Association for Computer Linguistics.

Akshay Krishna Sheshadri, Anvesh Rao Vijjini, and Sukhdeep Kharbanda. 2021. Wer-bert: Automatic wer estimation with bert in a balanced ordinal classification paradigm.

Ashish Vaswani, Noam Shazeer, Niki Parmar, Jakob Uszkoreit, Llion Jones, Aidan N. Gomez, Lukasz Kaiser, and Illia Polosukhin. 2017. Attention is all you need. In *Advances in Neural Information Processing Systems 30: Annual Conference on Neural Information Processing Systems 2017, December 4-9, 2017, Long Beach, CA, USA*, pages 5998–6008.

Ruiqing Zhang, Xiyang Wang, Chuanqiang Zhang, Zhongjun He, Hua Wu, Zhi Li, Haifeng Wang, Ying Chen, and Qinfei Li. 2021. Bstc: A large-scale chinese-english speech translation dataset. *arXiv preprint arXiv:2104.03575*.

BSTC: A Large-Scale Chinese-English Speech Translation Dataset

Ruiqing Zhang, Xiyang Wang, Chuanqiang Zhang, Zhongjun He
Hua Wu, Zhi Li, Haifeng Wang, Ying Chen, Qinfei Li
Baidu Inc. No. 10, Shangdi 10th Street, Beijing, 100085, China
{zhangruiqing01, zhangchuanqiang, hezhongjun, wu_hua}@baidu.com

Abstract

This paper presents BSTC (Baidu Speech Translation Corpus), a large-scale Chinese-English speech translation dataset. This dataset is constructed based on a collection of licensed videos of talks or lectures, including about 68 hours of Mandarin data, their manual transcripts and translations into English, as well as automated transcripts by an automatic speech recognition (ASR) model. We have further asked three experienced interpreters to simultaneously interpret the testing talks in a mock conference setting. This corpus is expected to promote the research of automatic simultaneous translation as well as the development of practical systems. We have organized simultaneous translation tasks and used this corpus to evaluate automatic simultaneous translation systems.

1 Introduction

In recent years, automatic speech translation (AST) has attracted increasing interest for its commercial potential (*e.g., Simultaneous Interpretation* and *Wireless Speech Translator*). A large amount of research has focused on speech translation (Weiss et al., 2017; Niehues et al., 2018; Chung et al., 2018; Sperber et al., 2019; Kahn et al., 2020; Inaguma et al., 2020) and simultaneous translation (Sridhar et al., 2013; Oda et al., 2014; Cho and Esipova, 2016; Gu et al., 2017; Ma et al., 2019; Arivazhagan et al., 2019; Zhang et al., 2020). The former intends to convert speech signals in the source language to the target language, and the latter aims to achieve a real-time translation that delivers the speech to the audience in the target language while minimizing the delay between the speaker and the translation.

To train an AST model, existing corpora can be classified into two categories:

- ***Speech Translation*** corpora consist pairs of audio segments and their corresponding translations.

Speech Translation	**Languages**	**Hours**
F-C (2013)	Es→En	38
KIT-Disfluency (2014)	De→En	13
BTEC (2016)	En→Fr	17
MSLT V1.0 (2016)	En↔Fr/De	23
	En→Zh/Jp	6
MSLT V1.1 (2017)	Zh→En	5
	Jp →En	9
Travel (2017)	Am→En	8
Aug-LibriSpeech (2018)	En→Fr	236
MuST-C (2019)	En→8 Euro langs	3617
Europarl-ST (2020)	9 Euro langs	1642
Covost (2020a; 2020b)	En↔21 langs	2880
Simultaneous Translation	**Languages**	**Hours**
CIAIR (2004)	En↔Jp	182
EPPS (2009)	En↔Es	217
Simul-Trans (2014)	En↔Jp	22
BSTC (ours)	Zh→En	68

Table 1: Existing speech translation corpora and ours. The duration statistics of all datasets are rounded up to an integer hour. For MuST-C, the "8 Euro langs" is short for "8 European languages". Europarl-ST contains the speech translation between 9 European languages.

- ***Simultaneous Translation*** corpora are constructed by transcribing lecturers' speeches and the streaming utterance of human interpreters.

The main difference between these two kinds of corpora lies in the way that the translations are generated. The translations in *Speech Translation* corpora are generated based on complete audios or their transcripts, while the translations in *Simultaneous Translation* corpora are transcribed from real-time human interpretation.

Existing research on *Speech Translation* mainly focused on the translation between English and Indo-European languages[1], with little attention paid to that between Chinese (Zh) and English. One of the reasons is the scarcity of public Zh↔En

[1] Indo-European languages are a large language family.

Proceedings of the 2nd Workshop on Automatic Simultaneous Translation, pages 28–35
June 10, 2021. ©2021 Association for Computational Linguistics

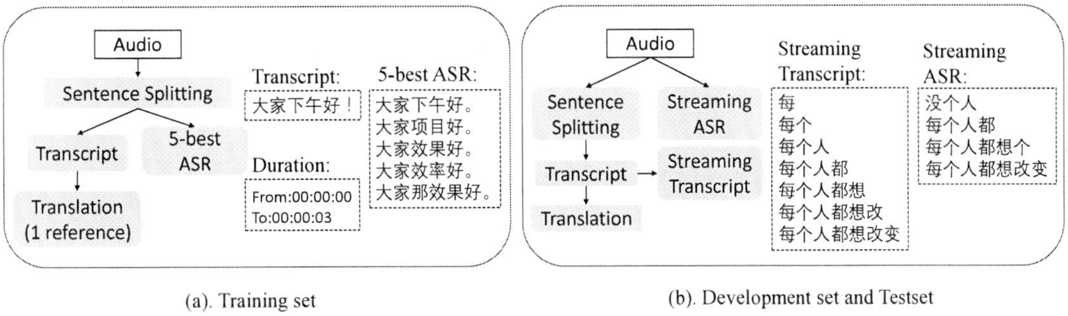

Figure 1: The process of constructing the training set and development/test sets (dev/test). The difference between the two processes is that for the training set we first split audio into sentences and then get the ASR and transcript for each sentence, while for the dev/test sets we record the real-time ASR and transcript, the sentence splitting is only used to generate translations of segmented sentences.

speech translation corpora. Among the public corpora, only MSLT (Federmann and Lewis, 2017) and Covost (Wang et al., 2020a,b) contains Zh↔En speech translation, as shown in Table 1. But the total volume of them on Zh→En translation is merely about 30 hours, which is too small to train data-hungry neural models. Some studies explore Zh→En *Simultaneous Translation* (Ma et al., 2019; Zhang et al., 2020). However, they take text translation datasets to simulate real-time translation scenarios because of the lack of simultaneous translation corpus.

To promote the research on Chinese-English speech translation, as well as evaluating the translation quality in real simultaneous interpretation environments, we construct BSTC, a large-scale Zh→En speech translation and simultaneous translation dataset including approximately 68 hours of Mandarin speech data with their automatic recognition results, manual transcripts, and translations. Our contributions are:

- We propose the first large-scale (68 hours) Chinese-English *Speech Translation* corpus. This training set is a four-way parallel dataset of Mandarin audio, transcripts, ASR lattices, and translations.
- The proposed dev and test set constitutes the first high-quality *Simultaneous Translation* dataset of over 3-hour Mandarin speech, together with its streaming transcript, streaming ASR results, and high-quality translation.
- We have organized two simultaneous interpretation tasks[2] to promote research in this field and deployed a strong benchmark on this dataset.
- The proposed dataset can also be taken as 1) a *Chinese Spelling error Correction* (CSC) corpus containing pairs of ASR results and corresponding manual transcripts or 2) a Zh→En *Document Translation* dataset with context-aware translations.

2 Dataset Description

BSTC is created to fill the gap in Zh→En speech translation, in terms of both size and quality. To achieve these objectives, we start by collecting approximate 68 hours of mandarin speeches from three TED-like content producers: BIT[3], *tndao.com*[4], and *zaojiu.com*[5]. The speeches involve a wide range of domains, including IT, economy, culture, biology, arts, etc. We randomly extract several talks from the dataset and divide them into the development and test set.

2.1 Training set

For the training set, we manually tag timestamps to split the audio into sentences, transcribe each sentence and ask professional translators to produce the English translations. The translation is generated based on the understanding of the entire talk and is faithful and coherent as a whole. To facilitate the research on robust speech translation, we also provide the top-5 ASR results for each segmented speech produced by SMLTA[6], a streaming multi-

[2]We organized two shared tasks on the 1st and 2nd Workshop on Automatic Simultaneous Translation.

[3]https://bit.baidu.com

[4]http://www.tndao.com/about-tndao

[5]https://www.zaojiu.com/

[6]http://research.baidu.com/Blog/index-view?id=109

Dataset	Talks	Utterances	Transcription (characters)	Translation (tokens)	Audio (hours)	WER(1-best)
Train	215	37,901	1,028,538	606,584	64.57	27.90%
Dev	16	956	26,059	75,074	1.58	15.21%
Test	6	975	25,832	70,503	1.46	10.32%

Table 2: The summary of our proposed speech translation data.

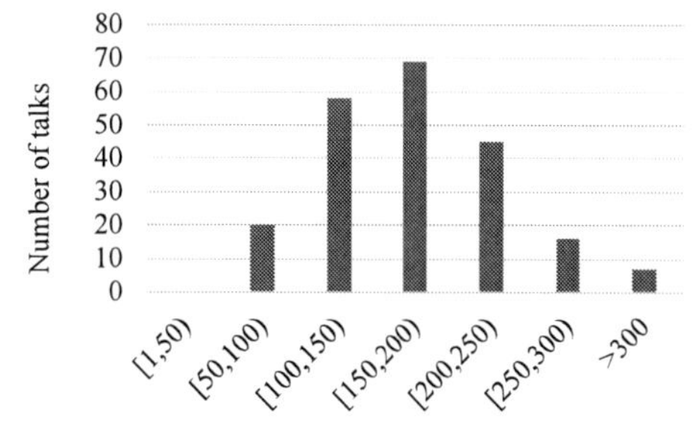

Figure 2: The distribution of talk length (number of sentences) in the training set.

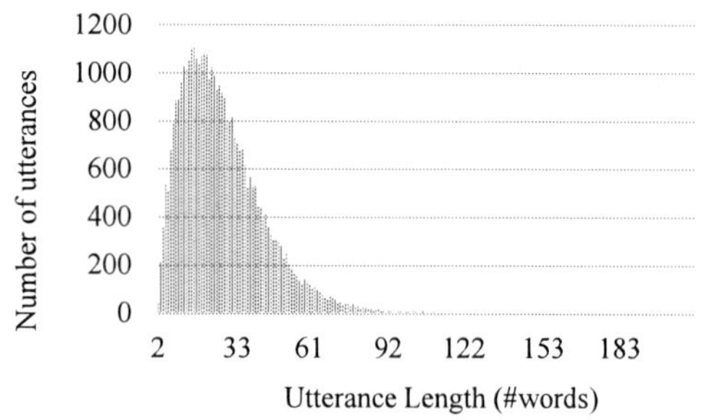

Figure 3: The distribution of utterance length (number of words) in the training set. A word means a Chinese character here.

layer truncated attention ASR model. Figure 1 (a) shows the construction process of the training set, together with an example of a segmented sentence.

2.2 Dev/Test set

For the development (dev) set and test set, we consider the simultaneous translation scenario and provide the streaming transcripts and streaming ASR results, as shown in Figure 1 (b). The streaming transcripts are produced by turning each n-words (a word means a Chinese character here) sentence to n lines word by word with length $1, 2, ..., n$. We use the real-time recognition results of each speech, rather than the recognition of each sentence-segmented audio. This is to simulate the simultaneous interpreting scenario, in which the input is streaming text, rather than segmented sentences.

d_{len}	WER	Coverage
0	5.87%	31.61%
1	7.13%	55.30%
3	8.86%	68.50%
7	10.72%	74.50%
15	15.23%	83.40%
31	23.51%	94.00%
∞	27.90%	100%

Table 3: The WER and coverage of different subsets of the training set with the length difference Δ_{len} between transcript and asr lower than or equal to d_{len}.

2.3 Statistics and Dataset Features

We summarize the statistics of our dataset in Table 2. The distribution of talk length and utterance length in the training set is illustrated in Figure 2 and Figure 3, respectively. The average number of utterances per talk is 176.3 in the training set, 59.8 in the dev set, and 162.5 in the test set. And the average utterance length is 27.14 in the training set, 27.26 in the dev set, and 26.49 in the test set.

We also calculate the word error rate[7] (WER) of the ASR system on the three datasets. As shown in Table 2, the WER of the training set is 27.90%, significantly higher than that of the dev and testset. This is due to the way of audio segmentation before recognition: some audio clips lose some parts in acoustic truncation, resulting in incomplete ASR results. We count the length difference of each <transcription, asr> pair, i.e., $\Delta_{len} = |len(transcription) - len(asr)|$, and recalculate the WER of pairs whose length difference is within a certain range. The WER and coverage of these subsets are listed in Table 3. Note that when the asr and transcript with equal length ($\Delta_{len} \leq 0$), the WER is only 5.87%. For the length difference in a relatively regular range (e.g, $\Delta_{len} \leq 15$), the WER is also relatively low (WER=15.23%).

Besides, there is a difference between our dataset and the existing speech translation corpora. In our dataset, speech irregularities are kept in transcrip-

[7]WER tool: `https://github.com/belambert/asr-evaluation`

	BLEU	AP	Omissions
A	24.20	83.0%	53%
B	17.14	62.8%	47%
C	25.18	76.5%	53%

Table 4: Comparison of the simultaneous interpretation results of three interpreters (A, B, and C) on the BSTC test set. "AP" is the Acceptability and the "Omissions" indicates the proportion of missing translation in all translation errors.

tion while omitted in translation (eg. filler words like "嗯, 呃, 啊", unconscious repetitions like "这个这个呢" and some disfluencies), which can be used to evaluate the robustness of the NMT model dealing with spoken language. Some other large-scale speech translation datasets (Kocabiyikoglu et al., 2018; Di Gangi et al., 2019), on the contrary, ignore these speech irregularities in the transcript.

2.4 Human Interpretation

We further ask three experienced interpreters (A, B, and C) with interpreting experience ranging from four to nine years to interpret the six talks of the testset, in a mock conference setting[8].

To evaluate their translation quality, we also ask human translators to evaluate the transcribed interpretation from multiple aspects: adequacy, fluency, and correctness:

- **Rank1**: The translation contains no obvious errors.
- **Rank2**: The translation is comprehensible and adequate, but with minor errors such as incorrect function words and less fluent phrases.
- **Rank3**: The translation is incorrect and unacceptable.

Table 4 shows the translation quality in BLEU and acceptability, which is calculated as the sum of the percentages of Rank1 and Rank2. It shows that their acceptability ranges from 62.8% to 83.0%, but the acceptability and BLEU are not completely positively correlated. This is because human interpreters routinely omit less important information to overcome their limitations in working memory. Acceptability focuses more on accuracy and faithfulness than adequacy, so it can tolerate information omission. Therefore, some information omitted in human interpretation that results in inferior BLEU may not lead to the decrease of acceptability. But BLEU, as a statistical auto-evaluation metric, considers adequacy with the same importance with accuracy. This leads to the discrepancy between BLEU and acceptability.


```
{
"offset": "105.975",
"duration": "3.287",
"wav": "2.wav",
"transcript": "但是你们的每个人都有多个设备，啊有手持
              设备，有手机。",
"Streaming ASR":
        Type: partial  但是
        Type: partial  但是你们
        Type: partial  但是你们的没
        Type: partial  但是你们的没个人都
        Type: partial  但是你们的没个人都有多个
        Type: final    但是你们的没个人都有多个设备
        Type: partial  啊有
        Type: partial  啊有首
        Type: partial  啊有手持摄
        Type: final    啊有手持设备
        Type: partial  首
        Type: partial  手机

"translation": "In fact, every one of you has multiple digital devices,
               handheld devices and mobile phones.",
"interpreter A": "But actually you own several devices, mobile devices,
                 mobile phones.",
"interpreter B": "But every of you have multiple equipments with you
                 hand held equipment like phone, smartphone.",
"interpreter C": "But every one of you have multi devices, we have
                 mobile phones."
}
```


Figure 4: A segment of one example in our test set, including audio, timelines, transcription, translation, streaming ASR results, and interpretation from three human interpreters (only for testing data). The red characters in "Streaming ASR" indicate recognition errors.

Figure 4 lists a segment from one example in our dataset. Notably, we only supply human interpretations for testing data. Here the "Streaming ASR" is the real-time recognition results, in which the "Type:final" means that the audio has detected a pause or silence and thus segmented, and will start to recognize a new sentence, while "Type:partial" is to continue recognizing the current sentence.

3 Experiments

In this section, we introduce our benchmark systems based on the dataset. We conduct experiments on speech translation and simultaneous translation, respectively.

To preprocess the Chinese and the English text, we use an open-source Chinese Segmenter[9], and Moses Tokenizer[10]. After tokenization, we convert

[8]We play the video of the speech, just like in a real simultaneous interpretation scene

[9]https://github.com/fxsjy/jieba

[10]https://github.com/moses-smt/mosesdecoder/blob/master/scripts/

Systems	Test on Transcript		Test on ASR	
	Dev	Test	Dev	Test
pre-train on WMT	20.78	35.13	18.22	33.32
Finetune on <transcript, translation>	**23.47**(2.69↑)	**41.14**(6.01↑)	19.68(1.46↑)	35.71(2.39↑)
Finetune on <ASR, translation>	22.53(1.75↑)	39.23(4.1↑)	**19.82**(1.6↑)	**36.89**(3.57↑)

Table 5: The results of benchmark trained on different training datasets, and evaluated by streaming transcription and ASR input.

all English letters into lower case. To train the MT model, we conduct byte-pair encoding (Sennrich et al., 2016) for both Chinese and English by setting the vocabulary size to 20K and 18K for Chinese and English, respectively. And we use the "multi-bleu.pl" [11] script to evaluate the BLEU score.

3.1 Benchmark System

Our benchmark is a cascade system that includes an ASR module, a sentence segmentation module, and a machine translation (MT) module.

- We use the SMLTA model for ASR, i.e., the streaming transcript/ASR of BSTC is taken as the output of the ASR module.
- The sentence segmentation module is to decide when to translate in real-time. We train a classification model based on the Meaningful Unit (MU) method proposed in Zhang et al. (2020) that implements a 5-class classification (MU, comma, period, question mark, and none). The training data of meaningful units are generated automatically from monolingual sentences based on context-aware translation consistency. The model is pre-trained on ERNIE-base (Sun et al., 2020) and fine-tuned on the transcript of the BSTC training set.
- Once an MU or a sentence boundary (period or question mark) is detected in the sentence segmentation module, the MT module generates translation for the detected sentence. The MT model is firstly pre-trained on the large-scale WMT19 Chinese-English corpus, then fine-tuned on BSTC. The WMT19 corpus includes 9.1 million sentence pairs collected from different sources, *i.e.*, Newswire, United Nations Parallel Corpus, Websites, etc. We use the *big* version of Transformer model in the following experiments.

tokenizer/tokenizer.perl

[11]https://github.com/moses-smt/\mosesdecoder/blob/master/scripts/generic/multi-bleu.perl

3.2 Performance of Speech Translation

Speech translation aims at translating accurately without considering system delay. Therefore, we only perform translation when sentence boundaries (periods and question marks) are detected by the sentence segmentation module.

The MT model is firstly trained on WMT, then fine-tuned on 37,901 training pairs of <transcription, translation> and <asr, translation> in two settings, respectively. The purpose of fine-tuning on transcription is to adapt the model to the speech domain, and the purpose of fine-tuning on ASR is to improve the robustness of the MT model against recognition errors. Our model pre-trained on WMT19 achieves a BLEU of 25.1 on Newstest19.

We evaluate our systems on the dev/test set using streaming transcription and streaming ASR as inputs. For each talk in the dev/test set, its streaming text is firstly segmented by the sentence segmentation module, then the translation of each segmentation is concatenated into one long sentence to evaluate the BLEU score. The results are listed in Table 5. Note that the great gap of BLEU in dev and test sets is that, the dev set has only one reference while the testset has 4 references.

Contribution of fine-tuning on speech translation data: The systems pre-trained on WMT obtain an absolute improvement both on clean and noisy input by fine-tuning on <transcription, translation>. The performance of the former model increases by 4.35 BLEU score on average and the latter model obtains 1.93 BLEU score improvement on average. This indicates the transcribed training data can still bring large improvement after pre-training on large-scale training corpus. This probably because it is closer to the test set in terms of the domain (speech) and noise (disfluencies in spoken language).

Contribution of fine-tuning on noisy data: Training on the corpus containing the ASR errors can be effective to improve the robustness of the NMT model. This can be proved by fine-tuning

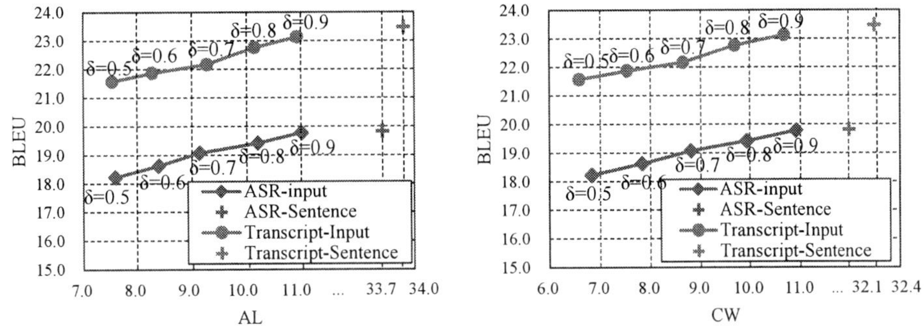

Figure 5: Translation quality against latency metrics on BSTC development set. "ASR-Sentence" and "Transcript-Sentence" denotes the results of full-sentence translation with ASR input and transcript input, respectively.

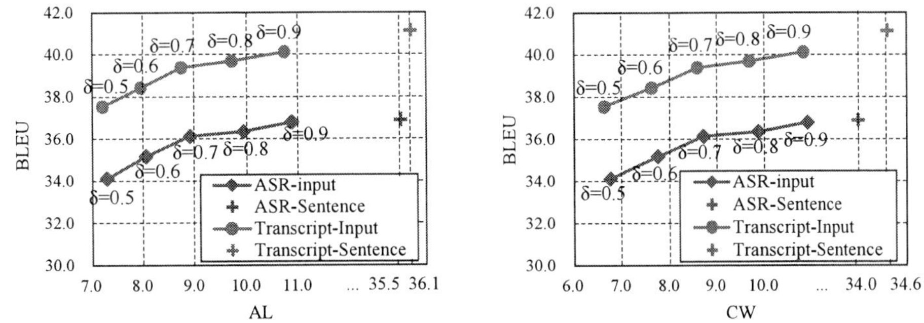

Figure 6: Translation quality against latency metrics on BSTC testset.

on the <ASR, translation> pairs. As shown in the last row of Table 5, the pre-trained model improves 2.93 and 2.59 BLEU scores on average for testing on streaming transcript and streaming ASR, respectively. This manifests that compared with fine-tuning the clean transcription, the model fine-tuned on ASR is less sensitive to false recognition results of ASR.

3.3 Performance of Simultaneous Translation

Different from speech translation, the simultaneous translation should balance translation quality and latency. Therefore, we fix the ASR and MT modules to evaluate our system under different sentence segmentation results. In simultaneous translation, once an MU or a sentence boundary is detected, the MU or sentence is translated immediately. In order to maintain coherent and consistent paragraph translation, we perform context-aware translation following Xiong et al. (2019) that except for the first segment in a sentence, the subsequent segments are translated with force-decoding.

The performance of system on the dev set and test set is listed in Figure 5 and Figure 6, respectively[12]. We use BLEU to evaluate the translation quality and use average lagging (AL) (Ma et al., 2019) and Consecutive Wait (CW) (Gu et al., 2017) as latency metrics. δ is the hyperparameter defined in Zhang et al. (2020) as the thresold of sentence segmentation module. It shows that the translation quality improves consistently with the increase of latency. The AL on both dev and test sets ranges from 7 to 12 and the CW ranges from 6 to 11 for points of simultaneous translation. In addition, we also draw the full-sentence translation results, as denoted by "ASR-Sentence" and "Transcript-Sentences" in the two figures. The full-sentence translation implements a high-latency policy, in which a translation is only triggered when a sentence is received. As shown in the figures, the delay of both "ASR-Sentence" and "Transcript-Sentences" is much higher than the simultaneous translation results.

4 Conclusion and Future Work

In this paper, we release a challenging dataset for the research on Chinese-English speech translation and simultaneous translation. Based on this

[12]We list detailed values in Table 6

	δ	AL	CW	BLEU
Dev Set	**Input ASR**			
	0.5	7.61	6.82	19.07
	0.6	8.42	7.83	19.42
	0.7	9.17	8.80	19.78
	0.8	10.26	9.94	20.25
	0.9	11.08	10.91	20.37
	Input Transcript			
	0.5	7.54	6.58	21.87
	0.6	8.30	7.54	22.16
	0.7	9.31	8.64	22.76
	0.8	10.19	9.70	23.13
	0.9	11.00	10.67	23.62
Test set	**Input ASR**			
	0.5	7.28	6.75	34.12
	0.6	8.04	7.75	35.18
	0.7	8.90	8.71	36.14
	0.8	9.93	9.88	36.35
	0.9	10.87	10.91	36.79
	Input Transcript			
	0.5	7.20	6.62	37.54
	0.6	7.94	7.61	38.43
	0.7	8.73	8.58	39.38
	0.8	9.70	9.70	39.69
	0.9	10.74	10.81	40.12

Table 6: Specific data corresponding to Figure 5 and Figure 6.

dataset, we report a competitive benchmark based on a cascade system. In the future, we will expand this dataset, and propose an effective method to develop an End-to-End speech translation model.

References

Naveen Arivazhagan, Colin Cherry, Wolfgang Macherey, Chung-Cheng Chiu, Semih Yavuz, Ruoming Pang, Wei Li, and Colin Raffel. 2019. Monotonic infinite lookback attention for simultaneous machine translation. In *Proceedings of the 57th Annual Meeting of the Association for Computational Linguistics*, pages 1313–1323, Florence, Italy. Association for Computational Linguistics.

Alexandre Bérard, Olivier Pietquin, Christophe Servan, and Laurent Besacier. 2016. Listen and translate: A proof of concept for end-to-end speech-to-text translation. *arXiv preprint arXiv:1612.01744*.

Eunah Cho, Sarah Fünfer, Sebastian Stüker, and Alex Waibel. 2014. A corpus of spontaneous speech in lectures: The KIT lecture corpus for spoken language processing and translation. In *Proceedings of the Ninth International Conference on Language Resources and Evaluation (LREC'14)*, pages 1554–1559, Reykjavik, Iceland. European Language Resources Association (ELRA).

Kyunghyun Cho and Masha Esipova. 2016. Can neural machine translation do simultaneous translation? *arXiv preprint arXiv:1606.02012*.

Yu-An Chung, Wei-Hung Weng, Schrasing Tong, and James Glass. 2018. Unsupervised cross-modal alignment of speech and text embedding spaces. *arXiv preprint arXiv:1805.07467*.

Mattia A Di Gangi, Roldano Cattoni, Luisa Bentivogli, Matteo Negri, and Marco Turchi. 2019. Must-c: a multilingual speech translation corpus. In *2019 Conference of the North American Chapter of the Association for Computational Linguistics: Human Language Technologies*, pages 2012–2017. Association for Computational Linguistics.

Christian Federmann and William D Lewis. 2016. Microsoft speech language translation (mslt) corpus: The iwslt 2016 release for english, french and german. In *International Workshop on Spoken Language Translation*.

Christian Federmann and William D Lewis. 2017. The microsoft speech language translation (mslt) corpus for chinese and japanese: conversational test data for machine translation and speech recognition. *Proceedings of the 16th Machine Translation Summit, Nagoya, Japan*.

Jiatao Gu, Graham Neubig, Kyunghyun Cho, and Victor OK Li. 2017. Learning to translate in real-time with neural machine translation. In *Proceedings of the 15th Conference of the European Chapter of the Association for Computational Linguistics: Volume 1, Long Papers*, pages 1053–1062.

Hirofumi Inaguma, Shun Kiyono, Kevin Duh, Shigeki Karita, Nelson Enrique Yalta Soplin, Tomoki Hayashi, and Shinji Watanabe. 2020. Espnet-st: All-in-one speech translation toolkit. *arXiv preprint arXiv:2004.10234*.

Javier Iranzo-Sánchez, Joan Albert Silvestre-Cerdà, Javier Jorge, Nahuel Roselló, Adrià Giménez, Albert Sanchis, Jorge Civera, and Alfons Juan. 2020. Europarl-st: A multilingual corpus for speech translation of parliamentary debates. In *ICASSP 2020-2020 IEEE International Conference on Acoustics, Speech and Signal Processing (ICASSP)*, pages 8229–8233. IEEE.

Jacob Kahn, Morgane Rivière, Weiyi Zheng, Evgeny Kharitonov, Qiantong Xu, Pierre-Emmanuel Mazaré, Julien Karadayi, Vitaliy Liptchinsky, Ronan Collobert, Christian Fuegen, et al. 2020. Libri-light: A benchmark for asr with limited or no supervision. In *ICASSP 2020-2020 IEEE International Conference on Acoustics, Speech and Signal Processing (ICASSP)*, pages 7669–7673. IEEE.

Ali Can Kocabiyikoglu, Laurent Besacier, and Olivier Kraif. 2018. Augmenting librispeech with french translations: A multimodal corpus for direct speech translation evaluation. *Language Resources and Evaluation*.

Mingbo Ma, Liang Huang, Hao Xiong, Kaibo Liu, Chuanqiang Zhang, Zhongjun He, Hairong Liu, Xing Li, and Haifeng Wang. 2019. STACL: simultaneous translation with integrated anticipation and controllable latency. In *ACL 2019*, volume abs/1810.08398.

Jan Niehues, Quan Pham, Thanh Le Ha, Matthias Sperber, and Alex Waibel. 2018. Low-latency neural speech translation. In *Interspeech 2018*, pages 1293–1297.

Yusuke Oda, Graham Neubig, Sakriani Sakti, Tomoki Toda, and Satoshi Nakamura. 2014. Optimizing segmentation strategies for simultaneous speech translation. In *Proceedings of the 52nd Annual Meeting of the Association for Computational Linguistics (Volume 2: Short Papers)*, volume 2, pages 551–556.

Matthias Paulik and Alex Waibel. 2009. Automatic translation from parallel speech: Simultaneous interpretation as mt training data. In *2009 IEEE Workshop on Automatic Speech Recognition & Understanding*, pages 496–501. IEEE.

Matt Post, Gaurav Kumar, Adam Lopez, Damianos Karakos, Chris Callison-Burch, and Sanjeev Khudanpur. 2013. Improved speech-to-text translation with the Fisher and Callhome Spanish–English speech translation corpus. In *Proceedings of the International Workshop on Spoken Language Translation (IWSLT)*, Heidelberg, Germany.

Rico Sennrich, Barry Haddow, and Alexandra Birch. 2016. Neural machine translation of rare words with subword units. In *Proceedings of the 54th Annual Meeting of the Association for Computational Linguistics (Volume 1: Long Papers)*, volume 1, pages 1715–1725.

Hiroaki Shimizu, Graham Neubig, Sakriani Sakti, Tomoki Toda, and Satoshi Nakamura. 2014. Collection of a simultaneous translation corpus for comparative analysis. In *LREC*, pages 670–673. Citeseer.

Matthias Sperber, Graham Neubig, Jan Niehues, and Alex Waibel. 2019. Attention-passing models for robust and data-efficient end-to-end speech translation. In *Transactions of the Association for Computational Linguistics*.

Vivek Kumar Rangarajan Sridhar, John Chen, Srinivas Bangalore, Andrej Ljolje, and Rathinavelu Chengalvarayan. 2013. Segmentation strategies for streaming speech translation. In *Proceedings of the 2013 Conference of the North American Chapter of the Association for Computational Linguistics: Human Language Technologies*, pages 230–238.

Yu Sun, Shuohuan Wang, Yukun Li, Shikun Feng, Hao Tian, Hua Wu, and Haifeng Wang. 2020. Ernie 2.0: A continual pre-training framework for language understanding. In *Proceedings of the AAAI Conference on Artificial Intelligence*, volume 34, pages 8968–8975.

Hitomi Tohyama, Shigeki Matsubara, Koichiro Ryu, N Kawaguch, and Yasuyoshi Inagaki. 2004. Ciair simultaneous interpretation corpus. In *Proc. Oriental COCOSDA*.

Changhan Wang, Juan Pino, Anne Wu, and Jiatao Gu. 2020a. Covost: A diverse multilingual speech-to-text translation corpus. *arXiv preprint arXiv:2002.01320*.

Changhan Wang, Anne Wu, and Juan Pino. 2020b. Covost 2: A massively multilingual speech-to-text translation corpus. *arXiv preprint arXiv:2007.10310*.

Ron J Weiss, Jan Chorowski, Navdeep Jaitly, Yonghui Wu, and Zhifeng Chen. 2017. Sequence-to-sequence models can directly translate foreign speech. *arXiv preprint arXiv:1703.08581*.

Michael Melese Woldeyohannis, Laurent Besacier, and Million Meshesha. 2017. A corpus for amharic-english speech translation: the case of tourism domain. In *International Conference on Information and Communication Technology for Develoment for Africa*, pages 129–139. Springer.

Hao Xiong, Ruiqing Zhang, Chuanqiang Zhang, Zhongjun He, Hua Wu, and Haifeng Wang. 2019. Dutongchuan: Context-aware translation model for simultaneous interpreting. *arXiv preprint arXiv:1907.12984*.

Ruiqing Zhang, Chuanqiang Zhang, Zhongjun He, Hua Wu, and Haifeng Wang. 2020. Learning adaptive segmentation policy for simultaneous translation. In *Proceedings of the 2020 Conference on Empirical Methods in Natural Language Processing (EMNLP)*, pages 2280–2289, Online. Association for Computational Linguistics.

Findings of the Second Workshop on Automatic Simultaneous Translation

Ruiqing Zhang, Chuanqiang Zhang, Zhongjun He, Hua Wu, Haifeng Wang
Baidu Inc. No. 10, Shangdi 10th Street, Beijing, 100085, China
{zhangruiqing01, zhangchuanqiang, hezhongjun, wu_hua}@baidu.com

Abstract

This paper presents the results of the shared task of the 2nd Workshop on Automatic Simultaneous Translation (AutoSimTrans). The task includes two tracks, one for text-to-text translation and one for speech-to-text, requiring participants to build systems to translate from either the source text or speech into the target text. Different from traditional machine translation, the AutoSimTrans shared task evaluates not only translation quality but also latency. We propose a metric "Monotonic Optimal Sequence" (MOS) considering both quality and latency to rank the submissions. We also discuss some important open issues in simultaneous translation.

1 Introduction

Simultaneous translation is to translate concurrently with the speech in the source language, aiming to obtain high translation quality with low latency. The concurrent comprehension and production process makes simultaneous translation an extremely challenging task for both human experts and machines. As a combination of machine translation (MT), automatic speech recognition (ASR), and text-to-speech synthesis (TTS), simultaneous translation still facing many problems to be studied in the research and application. To promote the development in this cutting-edge field, we conduct a shared task at the 2nd Workshop on Automatic Simultaneous Translation.

This year, we focus on Chinese-English simultaneous translation and set up two tracks:

1. **Text-to-text track**, where the participants are asked to submit systems that translate streaming input text in real-time. The input of this track is human-annotated transcripts in streaming format, in which every n-word sentence is broken into n lines of sequences whose length ranges from 1 to n, incremented by 1. We set up this track for two reasons. On the one hand, the difficulty of the task is reduced by removing the recognition of speech. On the other hand, participants can focus on text processing, such as segmentation and translation, without being influenced by ASR errors.
2. **Speech-to-text track**, where the submitted systems need to produce a real-time translation of the given audio.

We provide BSTC (Zhang et al., 2021) (Baidu Speech Translation Corpus) as the training data, which consists of about 68 hours of Mandarin speeches, together with corresponding transcripts, ASR results, and translations. In addition, participants can also use bilingual corpus provided by CCMT (China Conference on Machine Translation)[1]. We will describe the data in detail in Section 2.

One objective of the shared task is to explore the performance of state-of-the-art simultaneous translation systems. Traditional evaluation metrics, such as BLEU, only measure the translation quality, while recently proposed metrics, such as Consecutive Wait (CW) (Gu et al., 2017) and Average Lagging (AL) (Ma et al., 2019) focus on latency. So far as we know, there is no metric that evaluates both quality and delay.

We ask the participants to submit systems under different configurations to produce multiple translation results with varying latency. Then we plot each result in a quality-latency coordinate. Normally, a system is regarded as the best if all of its points are above others (Figure 1(a)). However, in most cases, their lines of points intersect with each other (Figure 1(b)).

To consider both quality and latency in ranking, we propose a ranking metric, Monotonic Optimal Sequence (MOS) (Section 3). The idea is to first

[1] http://sc.cipsc.org.cn/mt/conference/2021/

Proceedings of the 2nd Workshop on Automatic Simultaneous Translation, pages 36–44
June 10, 2021.

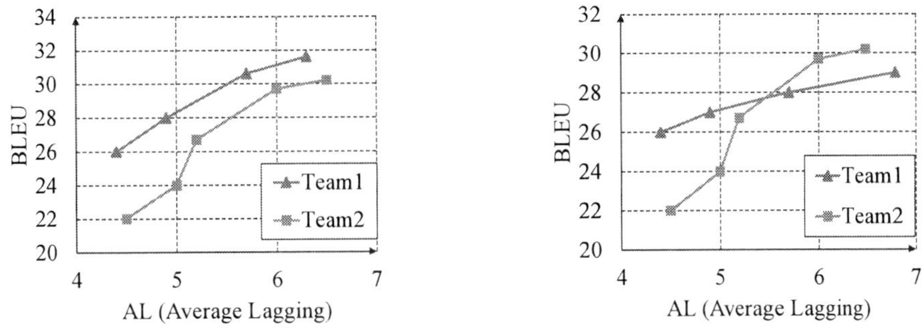

(a) (b)

Figure 1: Two examples of the results submitted by two teams. Each point shows the latency (X-axis) - BLEU (Y-axis) of a submitted system.

Corpus		Train	Dev	Test
BSTC	Audio (hours)	64.6	1.6	1.5
	#Talks	215	16	6
	#Utterances	37,901	956	975
CCMT	#Sentence Pairs	9.1M	2,000	/

Table 1: The summary of our provided corpora. The Dev set of CCMT2020 is Newstest2019. There are multiple test sets for CCMT so we don't list the statistics.

find all the optimal points, that is, a group of points with the highest quality under different latency, and then calculate the proportion of a system's optimal points in all its submitted points. The higher the proportion, the better the performance.

We received six submissions from four teams this year. We will report the results and analysis in Section 4. We discuss some important open issues in Section 5 and conclude the paper in Section 6.

2 Shared Task

We first introduce the data sets used in the shared task and the setup of the two tracks.

2.1 Training Set

Due to the scarcity of Zh→En speech translation corpora, we provide a Zh→En speech translation dataset BSTC and a large-scale text translation corpus CCMT for the participants.

- **BSTC** (Zhang et al., 2021) (Baidu Speech Translation Corpus) is a 68-hour Zh→En speech translation data including 215 speeches for training. Each speech is segmented into sentences, transcribed, and translated into English.
- We also encourage participants to use the large-scale Zh→En text translation corpus **CCMT 2020** (China Conference on Machine Translation) to enhance the performance of machine translation.

The statistics of the two datasets are listed in Table 1. As far as we know, BSTC is by far the largest Zh→En speech translation corpus, but it is still insufficient to train either a well-performed ASR model or an end-to-end simultaneous translation model in the speech-to-text track. Therefore, we don't impose restrictions on the dataset used by the participants for the speech track.

2.2 Test Set

Notice that the test set of BSTC shown in Table 1 is not released. The participants are required to submit docker systems, which will be tested on the 1.5-hours test set by us.

The test set is kept confidential as a progress test set. To validate the system to submit, we provide the dev set to the participants, which has the same format as the test set. It contains four-way parallel samples of 1) the streaming transcript, 2) the streaming asr, 3) the sentence-level translation of the transcript, and 4) the audio. The streaming transcripts are produced by turning each n-word (a word means a Chinese character here) sentence to n lines of word sequences with length 1, 2, ..., n. And the streaming ASR is produced by the real-time Baidu ASR system based on SMLTA[2].

2.3 Two Tracks

We set two tracks in our shared task, the text-to-text track is to input streaming transcripts and the

[2] http://research.baidu.com/Blog/index-view?id=109

speech-to-text track is to input audio files, as mentioned in section 1.

The simultaneous translation aims to balance system delay and translation quality. The key problem is to explore a policy that decides when to begin translating a source sentence before the speaker has finished his/her utterance. Eager policies, such as translating every word when it is received, will lead to poor translation quality, while lazy policies, such as waiting to translate until receiving a complete sentence, will result in long system delay.

In order to comprehensively evaluate each system's performance, we suggest that the participants generate multiple results on varying latency. Six systems from four teams were submitted in the shared task, four to Track 1 and two to Track 2.

3 System Evaluation

Unlike text translation evaluation that only takes one indicator (i.e., translation quality), simultaneous translation evaluation needs to consider quality and latency at the same time. The evaluation based on two criteria brings difficulties to ranking the systems. However, the two indicators are not easy to merge into one.

To rank the submissions better, we propose a ranking algorithm called Iterative Monotonic Optimal Sequence (I-MOS). Specifically, we define an *optimal point* as the result of the best translation quality at each latency. Our algorithm iteratively finds sets of optimal points to construct an optimal curve called Monotonic Optimal Sequence (MOS), then each team's proportion of points on the MOS curve is calculated to measure the performance. The overall process is illustrated in Figure 2.

In the following sections, we first introduce the commonly used metrics of quality and latency (Section 3.1), then propose the Monotonic Optimal Sequence (Section 3.2) and elaborate our I-MOS algorithm (Section 3.3).

3.1 Evaluation metrics

In simultaneous translation, quality is often measured by BLEU (Papineni et al., 2002). Recent work proposed some metrics for latency evaluation, such as Average Proportion (AP) (Cho and Esipova, 2016), Consecutive Wait (CW) (Gu et al., 2017), Average Lagging (AL) (Ma et al., 2019) and Differentiable Average Lagging (DAL) (Arivazhagan et al., 2019). Here we briefly introduce the two latency metrics used in our evaluation:

- **CW** is the average source segment length in words. It measures the number of source words being waited for between each two translation actions.
- **AL** quantifies the degree the audience is out of sync with the speaker by the average number of source words that the audience lags behind the ideal policy, in which the translation of each sentence is output at the same speed as the speaker's utterance and the entire translation finished when the speaker completes his/her utterance.

Note that the above-mentioned latency metrics are all proposed for text-to-text simultaneous translation and we use AL in the text track for latency evaluation. Some work extended AP and AL to speech translation (Ren et al., 2020; Ma et al., 2020), but we don't use them because they measure real-time latency, while some submissions calling remote services contain network delay. It is unreasonable to use real-time latency metrics for both the local-running systems and remote-running systems. Thus we ignore the latency of the ASR model and take the metrics of text-to-text simultaneous translation in the speech track. Specifically, we use BLEU-AL evaluation in the Text-to-text track and BLEU-CW evaluation in the Speech-to-text track.

3.2 Monotonic Optimal Sequence

To comprehensively rank systems based on the translation quality and latency, we propose to construct a monotonic optimal sequence composed of *Optimal Points*.

Definition 1. On the quality-latency figure, one result is considered optimal if there is no other point or line above it at an identical latency. In this case, the result is of the highest translation quality at that latency and we define it as an ***Optimal Point***.

For example, among the nine results of Figure 1 (b), the leftmost two points of Team1 and rightmost two points of Team2 are *Optimal Points*. The third point from left on Team2's curve is not optimal because it lies below the line of Team1.

To get *Optimal Points*, we select the results of the best translation quality with different latency. Since the submitted systems have discrete latency, we use the linear interpolation of adjacent points of each team to estimate their translation quality on continuous latency. Then we select some *Optimal Points* to form an optimal curve called Monotonic Optimal Sequence.

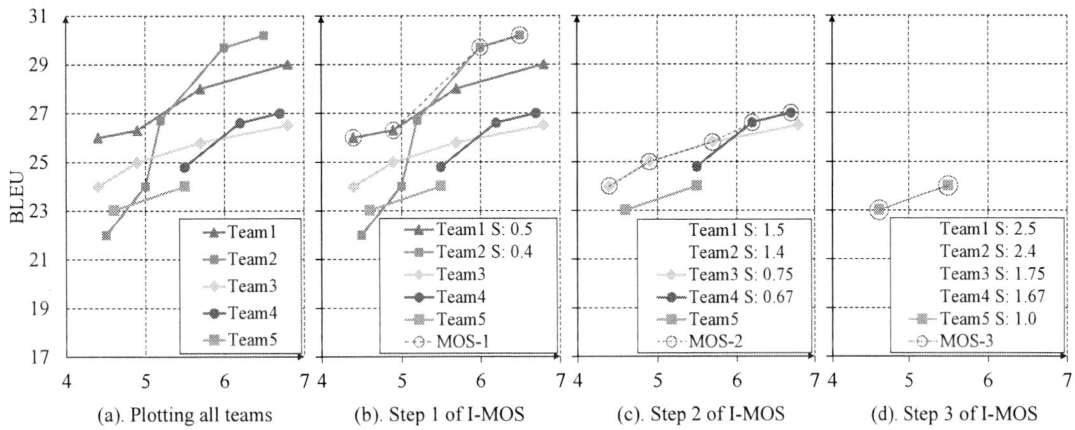

Figure 2: An illustration of our Iterative Monotonic Optimal Sequence (I-MOS) algorithm. First (a). plot the results of all teams, then (b) (c) (d) iteratively calculate the monotonic optimal sequence (MOS) of level k and update the score of the teams belong to level 1, 2, ..., k. The X-axis denotes the average lagging.

Definition 2. Let **Monotonic Optimal Sequence** (MOS) be a sequence of *Optimal Point* with increasing translation quality and latency.

We arrange all the *Optimal Points* in ascending order of latency and then select the points with monotonously increasing translation quality to form the MOS. The monotonicity requirement for translation quality is to avoid outlier points. For example, the rightmost point of Team1 in Figure 2 (b) is an outlier because there is no point or line above this point at the same latency, but it doesn't follow the monotonicity principle, so it should not be added to MOS.

We propose to use each team's proportion of points on the MOS to evaluate its performance. That is, we rank teams with:

$$S_{T_i} = \mathcal{N}(p^*_{t_i})/\mathcal{N}(p_{t_i}) \tag{1}$$

where $\mathcal{N}(p^*_{t_i})$ and $\mathcal{N}(p_{t_i})$ denote the number of points on MOS and the number of submitted points of team i, respectively. Therefore, the maximum value of S_{T_i} is 1, when all of its submitted points are on the MOS.

3.3 Iterative Monotonic Optimal Sequence Algorithm

There exists a problem in our measurement that, according to Eq. 1, all the teams that have no points on the MOS are ranked tied because they all score zero. To tackle this problem, we propose the Iterative Monotonic Optimal Sequence (I-MOS) algorithm. The main idea is to iteratively calculate the MOS curves, MOS-1, MOS-2, ... MOS-K, in which MOS-k denotes the Monotonic Optimal Sequence of level k calculated at the kth iteration. All the systems that have at least one point on MOS-k are classified to level k. We remove these systems and calculate MOS-$(k+1)$ in the next iteration. Each team of the kth level ranks higher than all teams of the $(k+1)^{th}$ level.

Our algorithm is elaborated in Algorithm 1. The level of all teams is initialized to zero (line 1), which denotes the team's score has not been calculated. Then we begin our iteration. While there exists at least one team whose score has not been calculated (line 4), we update the score of teams that belong to superior levels (level $1, 2, ..., k-1$) teams by adding the maximum value of S_{T_i} (1 point) to them (line 5-7) to ensure the systems of level $1, 2, ...k-1$ scores higher than systems of level k. Then we calculate MOS-k (line 8) and update the score of the teams that belong to level k according to Eq. 1 (line 9-11). After an iteration, we continue to explore teams that belong to level $k+1$ (line 12). Figure 2 provides a running process of I-MOS.

4 Systems Results

We received 6 systems submitted by four teams from four universities:

- Institute of computing technology, Chinese Academy of Science (ICT)
- Xiamen University (XMU)
- Beijing Institute of Technology (BIT)
- Ping An Technology (Shenzhen) Co., Ltd. (PingAn)

Algorithm 1: Iterative Monotonic Optimal Sequence (I-MOS)

```
Input: Number of teams N
Input: Teams submission: t_i contains all
       results submitted by team i
Output: Teams score S: s_i is the score of
        team i for ranking
tl = [0, 0, ..., 0]      ▷ Initialize teams level
        ▷ tl[i] denotes the level of team i
k ← 1                    ▷ Start from level 1
while ∏_{i=1}^{N} tl[i] = 0 do
    for i=1, 2, ..., N do
        if tl[i] ≠ 0 then
            s[i] ← s[i] + 1
    Calculate MOS-k   ▷ the k^th level MOS
    for i=1, 2, ..., N do
        if t_i has at least one point on MOS-k
        then
            tl[i] ← k
            s[i] ← N(p*_{t_i})/N(p_{t_i})
    k ← k + 1
```

Track 1		
Team Level	**Team**	$\mathcal{N}(p^*_{t_i})/\mathcal{N}(p_{t_i})$
Level 1	ICT	4/4
	XMU	2/3
	BIT	1/4
Level 2	PingAn	7/7
Track 2		
Level 1	PingAn	1/1
	XMU	1/3

Table 2: The evaluated level of each team and the proportion of points on the MOS of the corresponding level. The table shows the ranking of the teams from top to bottom.

We test each docker system with our testset, which contains 1.5 hours of 6 Mandarin talks. All the systems are run on V100 GPU. We plot the evaluation results in Figure 3 and rank them according to the I-MOS algorithm. Their ranking results are shown in Table 2. We use BLEU[3] to evaluate the translation quality and use Average Lagging (AL) (Ma et al., 2019) and Consecutive Wait (CW) (Gu et al., 2017) as latency metrics.

4.1 Text-to-text Track

In the first track, the results of the four teams reflect their preference in balancing system latency and translation quality. We briefly describe the methods of the four teams below in the order of their ranks:

1. **ICT** proposes the character-level *wait-k* policy, rather than using the standard word-level *wait-k* (Ma et al., 2019). They perform prefix-to-prefix MT training as in the original work. Besides, they follow the *multi-path* (Elbayad et al., 2020) and *future-guided* (Zhang et al., 2020b) methods to enhance the predictability and avoid huge anticipation in translation caused by *wait-k*. The *multi-path* method adopts randomly sampled k in $[1, 2, ..., K]$ in the training of incremental MT model to cover all possible k during training. And the *future-guided* method attempts to promote the prediction ability of the *wait-k* strategy. To improve the robustness of the MT model, they further try several data augmentation methods via adding noise to the source text.

2. **XMU** follows the *Meaningful Unit* (MU) segmentation policy proposed in Zhang et al. (2020a) that uses a context-aware classification model to determine whether the currently received ASR content can be definitely translated. To generate consistent translation given the segmentation, the MT model of the pipeline system is used to automatically generate training data of meaningful units. The MT model is trained by full-sentences pairs.

3. **BIT** uses a pipeline method with a segmentation model that bridges the streaming text input and the MT model. Once a punctuation mark is detected, the segmentation sends the currently received sub-sentence for translation as in (Zhang and Zhang, 2020). To make the MT model adapt to translating short sub-sentences at inference time, each sample in the provided parallel training corpus is automatically divided into multiple translation pairs for training. A statistical word alignment tool is used to segment the source sentence into minimal chunks so that crossing alignment links between source and target words occur only within individual chunks. The parallel pairs of chunks are then used to train their MT model.

[3]BLEU is calculated using " https://github.com/moses-smt/mosesdecoder/blob/master/scripts/generic/mteval-v13a.pl".

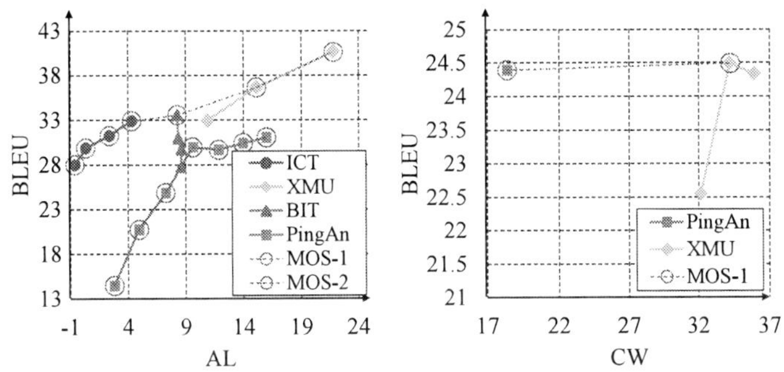

(a). Track1. Text-to-Text AST (b). Track2. Speech-to-Text AST

Figure 3: The evaluation results of the two tracks. The order in the legend denotes the real ranking.

4. **PingAn** takes the test-time *wait-k* (Ma et al., 2019) as the segmentation policy. Different from the standard *wait-k* policy, test-time *wait-k* uses the *wait-k* policy only at inference time without prefix-to-prefix training the MT model. They further adopt *Back-Translation* (Sennrich et al., 2016) to improve the translation quality.

In summary, we can categorize the four systems according to their segmentation policy: Both **ICT** and **PingAn** adopt the *wait-k* policy. **ICT** adopts training-time *wait-k* while **PingAn** uses test-time *wait-k*. **BIT** chooses sub-sentence translation, that is, to translate only when a punctuation is detected. **XMU** performs *MU-based* segmentation in which the training samples of meaningful units are generated by the MT model.

Figure 3 (a) shows that the latency of the two methods using *wait-k* is relatively low, while *MU-based* policy can achieve high translation quality. For the two *wait-k* systems, **ICT** performs better than **PingAn**, which is consistent with the experimental results in Ma et al. (2019) that training-time *wait-k* is superior to test-time *wait-k*.

It's interesting to find that the latency of **XMU** is larger than that of **BIT**. This might be because there are often long-distance reorderings in the training corpus. The reordering in translation that crosses punctuation marks would prevent the *MU* segmentation policy from extracting fine-grained MUs, resulting in the average length of *MU*s exceeding sub-sentences. This problem has been illustrated in Zhang et al. (2020a) and they proposed a refined method called *MU++* to alleviate the problem.

The result of **BIT** is a little weird. The translation quality decreases as system latency grows. This might be caused by the discrepancy between the segmentation module and the MT model. In their method, the segmentation module segments sentences into sub-sentences while the MT model is trained on statistically split chunks.

4.2 Speech-to-text Track

As elaborated in Section 3.1, we use BLEU and Consecutive Wait (CW) (Gu et al., 2017) to evaluate systems in the speech track.

PingAn and **XMU** continue their work based on their systems submitted to the Text-to-text track. The two systems both keep the same policy used in the first track and only replace the text input with the recognition results of an ASR model. **PingAn** trains a QuartzNet model (Kriman et al., 2020) with the Memory-Self-Attention (Luo et al., 2021) and **XMU** uses Baidu's real-time speech recognition service.

Figure 3 (b) shows that **PingAn** using wait-k outperforms **XMU** in latency. The reason behind the large delay of **XMU**'s system might be the same as in the first track.

5 Discussion

Most recent studies on simultaneous translation focused on methods to balance translation quality and latency. Besides this, we will discuss some other important challenges for simultaneous translation.

5.1 Data Scarcity

The first problem is the shortage of high-quality simultaneous translation data. In recent years, some speech translation corpora have released, such as MuST-C (Di Gangi et al., 2019), Covost (Wang et al., 2020a,b), Europarl-ST (Iranzo-Sánchez et al., 2020), Aug-LibriSpeech (Kocabiyikoglu et al., 2018), etc. These corpora focus on Indo-European

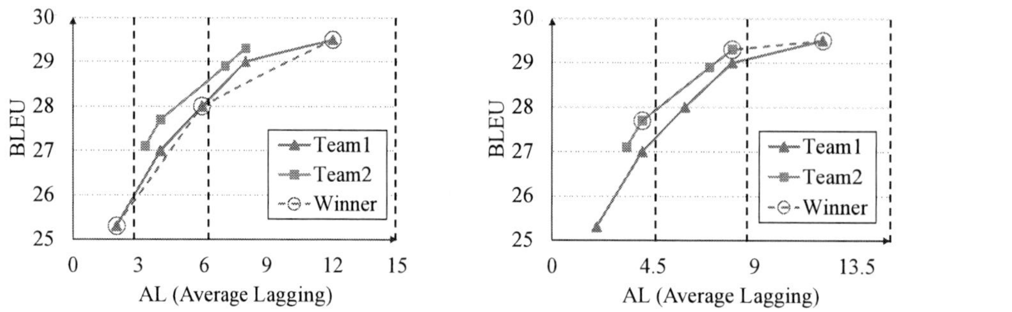

(a). IWSLT's Ranking with regimes boundary (3, 6, 15) (b). IWSLT's Evaluation with regimes boundary (4.5, 9, 13.5)

Figure 4: An illustration of the ranking algorithm of IWSLT's simultaneous translation shared task. The two figures vary only in the threshold of the latency regimes. According to their algorithm, the winner of figure (a) is Team1 in all the three regimes, while the winner evaluated in figure (b) is *Low Latency*: Team2, *Medium Latency*: Team2, and *High Latency*: Team1.

languages and have greatly contributed to the increasing popularity of research of simultaneous translation.

However, there is little attention paid to research and data collection of Chinese-English (Zh→En) simultaneous translation. To the best of our knowledge, only MSLT (Federmann and Lewis, 2016) and Covost (Wang et al., 2020b) contain Zh→En speech translation data, but they totally have about 30 hours of speech. In our shared task, we build 68-hour Zh→En speech translation corpus, BSTC (Zhang et al., 2021) for training and evaluation. The dataset alleviates the Zh→En data scarcity, but it's still insufficient to train data-hungry end-to-end simultaneous translation models.

5.2 Evaluation Dilemma

The second problem lies in system evaluation, which has not been widely explored.

Traditional metrics such as BLEU (Papineni et al., 2002), NIST (Doddington, 2002), METEOR (Banerjee and Lavie, 2005), etc, are designed for text translation. These metrics based on accurate matching between system outputs and references. However, to reduce latency in simultaneous interpretation, human interpreters usually use strategies such as reasonable omissions, avoiding long-distance reordering in translation, etc. Thus the traditional metrics are not suitable to evaluate the simultaneous interpretation.

On the other hand, there is no metric to evaluate both translation quality and latency. In our shared task, we propose a novel ranking algorithm, I-MOS. We only consider the proportion of *optimal points*, ignoring whether the points lie in low-latency or high-latency. Therefore, our ranking doesn't differentiate latency regimes. However, it remains open to question whether it is reasonable to compare two systems with no intersection in latency, like the **ICT** and **XMU** in Figure 3 (a). The ranking might be more convincing if **ICT** had provided results at high latency and **XMU** has provided results at low latency.

We note that IWSLT has also hosted simultaneous translation shared tasks[4]. They proposed to rank systems by the translation quality with different latency regimes: *Low Latency*: AL <= 3, *Medium Latency*: AL <= 6, and *High Latency*: AL <= 15. For each team, the submitted system that achieves the best translation quality is chosen for ranking in each latency regime. However, the value of artificially defined latency threshold between regimes has a big impact on the ranking results. As illustrated in Figure 4, different latency thresholds lead to completely different rankings of the two teams.

Actually, the ideal ranking mechanism is to rank all systems within a similar latency interval. However, asking participants to submit results in almost every latency regime is unreasonable, because existing policies all have a preference in trading off latency and translation quality. For example, *wait-k* focuses on getting controllable low latency, while the inspiration behind *MU* is to translate until a segment with definite meaning is formed, leading to a high latency as well as high quality. Therefore, it is a dilemma to evaluate systems comprehensively while distinguishing different latency regions reasonably. This problem can be explored in future

[4]https://iwslt.org/2021/simultaneous

work.

5.3 Applications

Recently, more and more simultaneous translation systems have emerged in international conferences.

In practical applications, systems face robust and controllability issues. Being robust denotes the system should achieve a high translation quality and be insensitive to speech noise, including sound capture noise, speaker's accent, disfluency in speech, etc. Being controllable means the system should be able to remember and understand some named entities and should be able to be intervened.

Our shared task provides such an opportunity for participants to pay attention to the robustness problem. For example, **ICT** and **PingAn** have adopted data augmentation to enhance the robustness of their systems.

In terms of controllability, it is not difficult to integrate an intervention mechanism in pipeline systems. For example, a pre-defined translation of a named entity can be introduced to the MT module. However, controllability is not easy to be guaranteed for end-to-end simultaneous translation systems (Ren et al., 2020; Ma et al., 2020). It remains a challenge to correct a translation without an intermediate ASR result. We also hope to see more work focusing on real-world simultaneous translation applications and discussing some interesting issues, such as the document-level ASR error correction in pipeline systems, and how to enhance the controllability in end-to-end speech-to-text systems, etc.

6 Conclusion

This paper presents the results of the Zh→En simultaneous translation shared task hosted on the 2nd Workshop on Automatic Simultaneous Translation (AutoSimTrans). The shared task includes two tracks, the text-to-text track (Track1) and the speech-to-text track (Track2). Six systems were submitted to the shared task, four to Track1 and two to Track2. We propose an evaluation method "Monotonic Optimal Sequence" (MOS) to evaluate both translation quality and time latency. We report the results and further discuss some important open issues of simultaneous translation.

Regrettably, the number of submissions is less than expected, especially for the speech-to-text track. In fact, there are more than 300 teams registered. However, most of them did not submit their results. The possible reason may be that the interdisciplinary task is not easy for participants. We hope to see more participants in the future.

References

Naveen Arivazhagan, Colin Cherry, Wolfgang Macherey, Chung-Cheng Chiu, Semih Yavuz, Ruoming Pang, Wei Li, and Colin Raffel. 2019. Monotonic infinite lookback attention for simultaneous machine translation. In *Proceedings of the 57th Annual Meeting of the Association for Computational Linguistics*, pages 1313–1323, Florence, Italy. Association for Computational Linguistics.

Satanjeev Banerjee and Alon Lavie. 2005. Meteor: An automatic metric for mt evaluation with improved correlation with human judgments. In *Proceedings of the acl workshop on intrinsic and extrinsic evaluation measures for machine translation and/or summarization*, pages 65–72.

Kyunghyun Cho and Masha Esipova. 2016. Can neural machine translation do simultaneous translation? *arXiv preprint arXiv:1606.02012.*

Mattia A Di Gangi, Roldano Cattoni, Luisa Bentivogli, Matteo Negri, and Marco Turchi. 2019. Must-c: a multilingual speech translation corpus. In *2019 Conference of the North American Chapter of the Association for Computational Linguistics: Human Language Technologies*, pages 2012–2017. Association for Computational Linguistics.

George Doddington. 2002. Automatic evaluation of machine translation quality using n-gram co-occurrence statistics. In *Proceedings of the second international conference on Human Language Technology Research*, pages 138–145.

Maha Elbayad, Laurent Besacier, and Jakob Verbeek. 2020. Efficient wait-k models for simultaneous machine translation. *arXiv preprint arXiv:2005.08595.*

Christian Federmann and William D Lewis. 2016. Microsoft speech language translation (mslt) corpus: The iwslt 2016 release for english, french and german. In *International Workshop on Spoken Language Translation.*

Jiatao Gu, Graham Neubig, Kyunghyun Cho, and Victor OK Li. 2017. Learning to translate in real-time with neural machine translation. In *Proceedings of the 15th Conference of the European Chapter of the Association for Computational Linguistics: Volume 1, Long Papers*, pages 1053–1062.

Javier Iranzo-Sánchez, Joan Albert Silvestre-Cerdà, Javier Jorge, Nahuel Roselló, Adrià Giménez, Albert Sanchis, Jorge Civera, and Alfons Juan. 2020. Europarl-st: A multilingual corpus for speech translation of parliamentary debates. In *ICASSP 2020-2020 IEEE International Conference on Acoustics, Speech and Signal Processing (ICASSP)*, pages 8229–8233. IEEE.

Ali Can Kocabiyikoglu, Laurent Besacier, and Olivier Kraif. 2018. Augmenting librispeech with french translations: A multimodal corpus for direct speech translation evaluation. *Language Resources and Evaluation*.

Samuel Kriman, Stanislav Beliaev, Boris Ginsburg, Jocelyn Huang, Oleksii Kuchaiev, Vitaly Lavrukhin, Ryan Leary, Jason Li, and Yang Zhang. 2020. Quartznet: Deep automatic speech recognition with 1d time-channel separable convolutions. In *ICASSP 2020-2020 IEEE International Conference on Acoustics, Speech and Signal Processing (ICASSP)*, pages 6124–6128. IEEE.

Jian Luo, Jianzong Wang, Ning Cheng, and Jing Xiao. 2021. Unidirectional memory-self-attention transducer for online speech recognition. *arXiv preprint arXiv:2102.11594*.

Mingbo Ma, Liang Huang, Hao Xiong, Renjie Zheng, Kaibo Liu, Baigong Zheng, Chuanqiang Zhang, Zhongjun He, Hairong Liu, Xing Li, et al. 2019. Stacl: Simultaneous translation with implicit anticipation and controllable latency using prefix-to-prefix framework. In *Proceedings of the 57th Annual Meeting of the Association for Computational Linguistics*, pages 3025–3036.

Xutai Ma, Juan Pino, and Philipp Koehn. 2020. Simulmt to simulst: Adapting simultaneous text translation to end-to-end simultaneous speech translation. *arXiv preprint arXiv:2011.02048*.

Kishore Papineni, Salim Roukos, Todd Ward, and Wei-Jing Zhu. 2002. Bleu: a method for automatic evaluation of machine translation. In *Proceedings of the 40th Annual Meeting of the Association for Computational Linguistics*, pages 311–318, Philadelphia, Pennsylvania, USA. Association for Computational Linguistics.

Yi Ren, Jinglin Liu, Xu Tan, Chen Zhang, QIN Tao, Zhou Zhao, and Tie-Yan Liu. 2020. Simulspeech: End-to-end simultaneous speech to text translation. In *Proceedings of the 58th Annual Meeting of the Association for Computational Linguistics*, pages 3787–3796.

Rico Sennrich, Barry Haddow, and Alexandra Birch. 2016. Improving neural machine translation models with monolingual data. In *Proceedings of the 54th Annual Meeting of the Association for Computational Linguistics (Volume 1: Long Papers)*, pages 86–96, Berlin, Germany. Association for Computational Linguistics.

Changhan Wang, Juan Pino, Anne Wu, and Jiatao Gu. 2020a. Covost: A diverse multilingual speech-to-text translation corpus. *arXiv preprint arXiv:2002.01320*.

Changhan Wang, Anne Wu, and Juan Pino. 2020b. Covost 2: A massively multilingual speech-to-text translation corpus. *arXiv preprint arXiv:2007.10310*.

Ruiqing Zhang, Xiyang Wang, Chuanqiang Zhang, Zhongjun He, Hua Wu, Zhi Li, ying Chen, and Qinfei Li. 2021. Bstc: A large-scale chinese-english speech translation dataset. In *Proceedings of the Second Workshop on Automatic Simultaneous Translation*. Association for Computational Linguistics.

Ruiqing Zhang and Chuanqiang Zhang. 2020. Dynamic sentence boundary detection for simultaneous translation. In *Proceedings of the First Workshop on Automatic Simultaneous Translation*, pages 1–9, Seattle, Washington. Association for Computational Linguistics.

Ruiqing Zhang, Chuanqiang Zhang, Zhongjun He, Hua Wu, and Haifeng Wang. 2020a. Learning adaptive segmentation policy for simultaneous translation. In *Proceedings of the 2020 Conference on Empirical Methods in Natural Language Processing (EMNLP)*, pages 2280–2289, Online. Association for Computational Linguistics.

Shaolei Zhang, Yang Feng, and Liangyou Li. 2020b. Future-guided incremental transformer for simultaneous translation. *arXiv preprint arXiv:2012.12465*.

Author Index

Association for Computational Linguistics
209 N. Eighth Street
Stroudsburg, Pennsylvania 18360

ISBN 978-1-7138-3016-0

CURRAN ASSOCIATES INC.
proceedings.com